THE GREAT
RECESSION
A Subversive View

T0314084

The Cañada Blanch / Sussex Academic Studies on Contemporary Spain

General Editor: Professor Paul Preston, London School of Economics

Margaret Joan Anstee, *JB – An Unlikely Spanish Don: The Life and Times of Professor John Brande Trend.*

Richard Barker, *Skeletons in the Closet, Skeletons in the Ground: Repression, Victimization and Humiliation in a Small Andalusian Town – The Human Consequences of the Spanish Civil War.*

Germà Bel, *Infrastructure and the Political Economy of Nation Building in Spain, 1720–2010.*

Gerald Blaney Jr., *"The Three-Cornered Hat and the Tri-Colored Flag": The Civil Guard and the Second Spanish Republic, 1931–1936.*

Michael Eaude, *Triumph at Midnight in the Century: A Critical Biography of Arturo Barea.*

Francisco Espinosa-Maestre, *Shoot the Messenger?: Spanish Democracy and the Crimes of Francoism – From the Pact of Silence to the Trial of Baltasar Garzón*

Soledad Fox, *Constancia de la Mora in War and Exile: International Voice for the Spanish Republic.*

María Jesús González, *Raymond Carr: The Curiosity of the Fox.*

Helen Graham, *The War and its Shadow: Spain's Civil War in Europe's Long Twentieth Century.*

Angela Jackson, *'For us it was Heaven': The Passion, Grief and Fortitude of Patience Darton – From the Spanish Civil War to Mao's China.*

Gabriel Jackson, *Juan Negrín: Physiologist, Socialist, and Spanish Republican War Leader.*

Sid Lowe, *Catholicism, War and the Foundation of Francoism: The Juventud de Acción Popular in Spain, 1931–1939.*

David Lethbridge, *Norman Bethune in Spain: Commitment, Crisis, and Conspiracy.*

Carles Manera, *The Great Recession: A Subversive View.*

Olivia Muñoz-Rojas, *Ashes and Granite: Destruction and Reconstruction in the Spanish Civil War and Its Aftermath.*

Linda Palfreeman, *¡SALUD!: British Volunteers in the Republican Medical Service during the Spanish Civil War, 1936–1939.*

Cristina Palomares, *The Quest for Survival after Franco: Moderate Francoism and the Slow Journey to the Polls, 1964–1977.*

David Wingeate Pike, *France Divided: The French and the Civil War in Spain.*

Hugh Purcell with Phyll Smith, *The Last English Revolutionary: Tom Wintringham, 1898–1949.*

Isabelle Rohr, *The Spanish Right and the Jews, 1898–1945: Antisemitism and Opportunism.*

Gareth Stockey, *Gibraltar: "A Dagger in the Spine of Spain?"*

Ramon Tremosa-i-Balcells, *Catalonia – An Emerging Economy: The Most Cost-Effective Ports in the Mediterranean Sea.*

Maria Thomas, *The Faith and the Fury: Popular Anticlerical Violence and Iconoclasm in Spain, 1931–1936.*

Dacia Viejo-Rose, *Reconstructing Spain: Cultural Heritage and Memory after Civil War.*

Richard Wigg, *Churchill and Spain: The Survival of the Franco Regime, 1940–1945.*

To
Joanet, Aineta, Carles,
Maria and Laia.

THE GREAT
RECESSION
A Subversive View

CARLES MANERA

sussex
ACADEMIC
PRESS
Brighton • Portland • Toronto

Cañada Blanch Centre
for Contemporary
Spanish Studies

2 4 6 8 10 9 7 5 3 1

Published in Catalan as *Capitalisme desfermat* (Palma: Lleonard Muntaner, 2012).
Published in English 2013 in Great Britain by
SUSSEX ACADEMIC PRESS
PO Box 139
Eastbourne BN24 9BP

and in the United States of America by
SUSSEX ACADEMIC PRESS
920 NE 58th Ave   Suite 300
Portland, Oregon 97213-3786

and in Canada by
SUSSEX ACADEMIC PRESS (CANADA)
8000 Bathurst Street, Unit 1, PO Box 30010, Vaughan, Ontario L4J 0C6

Translated by Timothy Barton (anglopremier.com) and revised by Steven Capsuto.

Published in collaboration with the
Cañada Blanch Centre for Contemporary Spanish Studies.

British Library Cataloguing in Publication Data
A CIP catalogue record for this book is available from the British Library.

Library of Congress Cataloging-in-Publication Data
Manera, Carles, 1957–
The great Recession : a subversive view / Carles Manera.
pages   cm
Includes bibliographical references and index.
ISBN 978-1-84519-603-5 (p/b : alk. paper)
   1. Financial crises. 2. Global Financial Crisis, 2008–2009. 3. Economic policy—History—21st century. I. Title.
HB3722.M33543 2013
330.9'051—dc23

2013006200

Typeset & designed by Sussex Academic Press, Brighton & Eastbourne.
Printed by TJ International, Padstow, Cornwall.

Contents

The Cañada Blanch Centre for Contemporary Spanish Studies

In the 1960s, the most important initiative in the cultural and academic relations between Spain and the United Kingdom was launched by a Valencian fruit importer in London. The creation by Vicente Cañada Blanch of the Anglo-Spanish Cultural Foundation has subsequently benefited large numbers of Spanish and British scholars at various levels. Thanks to the generosity of Vicente Cañada Blanch, thousands of Spanish schoolchildren have been educated at the secondary school in West London that bears his name. At the same time, many British and Spanish university students have benefited from the exchange scholarships which fostered cultural and scientific exchanges between the two countries. Some of the most important historical, artistic and literary work on Spanish topics to be produced in Great Britain was initially made possible by Cañada Blanch scholarships.

Vicente Cañada Blanch was, by inclination, a conservative. When his Foundation was created, the Franco regime was still in the plenitude of its power. Nevertheless, the keynote of the Foundation's activities was always a complete open-mindedness on political issues. This was reflected in the diversity of research projects supported by the Foundation, many of which, in Francoist Spain, would have been regarded as subversive. When the Dictator died, Don Vicente was in his seventy-fifth year. In the two decades following the death of the Dictator, although apparently indestructible, Don Vicente was obliged to husband his energies. Increasingly, the work of the Foundation was carried forward by Miguel Dols whose tireless and imaginative work in London was matched in Spain by that of José María Coll Comín. They were united in the Foundation's spirit of open-minded commitment to fostering research of high quality in pursuit of better Anglo-Spanish cultural relations. Throughout the 1990s, thanks to them, the role of the Foundation grew considerably.

In 1994, in collaboration with the London School of Economics, the Foundation established the Príncipe de Asturias Chair of Contemporary Spanish History and the Cañada Blanch Centre for Contemporary Spanish Studies. It is the particular task of the Cañada Blanch Centre for Contemporary Spanish Studies to promote the understanding of twentieth century Spain through research and teaching of contemporary Spanish history, politics, economy, sociology and culture. The Centre possesses a valuable library and archival centre for specialists in contemporary Spain. This work is carried on through the publications of the doctoral and post-doctoral researchers at the Centre itself and through the many seminars and lectures held at the London School of Economics. While the seminars are the province of the researchers, the lecture cycles have been the forum in which Spanish politicians have been able to address audiences in the United Kingdom.

Since 1998, the Cañada Blanch Centre has published a substantial number of books in collaboration with several different publishers on the subject of contemporary Spanish history and politics. A fruitful partnership with Sussex Academic Press began in 2004. Full details and descriptions of the published works can be found on the Press website. The present volume is a fascinating and original analysis of the great economic crisis that began five years ago. Carles Manera sees it as more than a problem of the financial system and widens his perspective to examine such factors as overproduction, falling business profits and environmental issues. His suggestions in terms of solutions go beyond the austerity proposed by the German and British governments. This is a subversive book about a European problem viewed from a Spanish standpoint.

Preface

This is the English-language version of a book I published in Catalan under the title *Capitalisme desfermat: Una visió subversiva sobre la Gran Recessió, 2008–2011* (Palma: Lleonard Muntaner Editor, 2012). The work looks at the Great Recession using bibliographical material and analysing publicly available data published by major institutions. I have tried to offer a different perspective on this major economic crisis, bearing in mind that changes to economics are coming thick and fast. The discourse I defend in this book aims to emphasise in particular the more permanent aspects of this turbulent world. But I am well aware that the traits of the Great Recession are prone to sudden changes, which often forces social scientists to adjust parts of diagnoses they have already given.

My research and writing was helped by spending a semester as a visiting lecturer at the University of Barcelona (UB) from September 2011 to February 2012, thanks to an invitation by the Department of History and Economic Institutions. I would like to express my thanks in particular to the lecturers Jordi Nadal (a long-standing major figure), Francesc Valls, Jordi Catalan, Carles Sudrià and Ricard Soto. I am especially grateful to the Head of Department Prof. Enric Tello and the lecturer Àlex Sánchez Suárez, as these colleagues and friends paved the way for my stay in Barcelona. The London School of Economics (LSE) has accepted me as a visiting researcher for 2012/13, thanks to the generosity of Prof. Paul Preston, an admirable historian and researcher to whom I owe a huge debt of gratitude. I am also indebted to Ana de Miguel, whose support and assistance was crucial, in every sense of the word, to my stay in London. Dídac Gutiérrez-Peris and Susana Grau have always given me all kinds of practical guidance and enabled me to surmount any administrative and technical difficulties.

The lecturers Gabriel Jover, Ramon Molina, Antònia Morey, Ferran Navinés and Andreu Sansó provided comments on drafts of the text, helping to improve the final version. I'm also thankful to

Miquel Quetglas for his generous work helping me compile statistics from the databases of the Spanish and Balearic statistics institutions, the IMF, the OECD and the European Commission. The meticulous work of the translator, Timothy Barton (anglopremier.com), was crucial, and his comments helped improve the text. I am also thankful to Steven Capsuto, who worked with the translator as proofreader and editor. My heartfelt thanks to you both.

The book is split into five chapters. Chapter 1 provides an introduction, outlining how the text will develop and plainly setting out the ideological standpoint adopted. Chapter 2 analyses the crisis, understood as a cyclical rather than a one-off event. It highlights some clearly essential elements: the loss of capacity of the US economy, the emergence of new competitors in international trade and the causes and characteristics of the crisis that broke out in 2008. Chapter 3 compares the orthodox and heterodox positions regarding how economic activity should be managed and looks at some of their key indicators, such as inflation, unemployment and growth variables. It also looks at profits, an essential factor in understanding that the crisis is not just financial, but that it also contains elements related to capitalist overproduction that can be observed in economic history. Chapter 4 underlines the role that a historical perspective can play and explores factors affecting the dominant ideology in economics, an ideology that ignores past experience and focuses uniquely on the most short-term factors. Based on a review of economic history, I propose several strategic objectives for economics, which suggest current and future lines of research. The final chapter provides some summarising thoughts that require specific actions to be carried out and outline new explanatory frameworks. The book closes with seven major empirical and theoretical considerations put forward in a provocative manner with the aim of sparking a debate on how economic and social policy (i.e. the growth model) should move forward in the world. It is an exercise in subversion that is increasingly necessary given the one-dimensional, heated, Orwellian discourse that is pointing the world towards depression, discouragement and paralysis.

CARLES MANERA
London–Palma, February 2013

Acknowledgements

I would also like to express my sincere thanks to various organisations and people who were essential in enabling this book to be published: Fernando Alzamora, Chairman of Caixa de Balears, Sa Nostra; Pau Dols, CEO of Caixa de Balears, Sa Nostra; Juan Ramón Fuertes, Balearic Islands Regional Director at La Caixa; Biel Roca and Jaume Julià, of Cajamar Caja Rural. I am also thankful for the vital co-operation of Alejandro Forcades, Chairman of the *Cercle d'Economia*; Miguel José Deyá, General Director of University for the Balearic Islands government; and Montserrat Casas, University President of the Universitat de les Illes Balears. Thank you to you all.

List of Tables and Figures

Utilitarian economists, . . . Commissioners of Fact, genteel and used-up infidels, . . . the poor you will have always with you. Cultivate in them, while there is yet time, the utmost graces of the fancies and affections, . . . when romance is utterly driven out of their souls, . . . Reality will take a wolfish turn, and make an end of you.

CHARLES DICKENS, 1854

I confess I am not charmed with the ideal of life held out by those who think that the normal state of human beings is that of struggling to get on; that the trampling, crushing, elbowing, and treading on each other's heels . . . are the most desirable lot of human kind. . . . I know not why it should be matter of congratulation that persons who are already richer than any one needs to be, should have doubled their means of consuming things. . . . It is scarcely necessary to remark that a stationary condition of capital and population implies no stationary state of human improvement. There would be as much scope as ever for all kinds of mental culture, and moral and social progress; as much room for improving the Art of Living, and much more likelihood of its being improved, when minds ceased to be engrossed by the art of getting on.

JOHN STUART MILL, 1857

Insanity is doing the same thing over and over again and expecting different results.

ALBERT EINSTEIN

With notably rare exceptions (2008, for example), the global "invisible hand" has created relatively stable exchange rates, interest rates, prices, and wage rates.

ALAN GREENSPAN, 2011

It is better to leave our children and our children's children an educated country than a debt-free country.

JOEL MOKYR, 2007

Our baseline scenario is that we will have a trough in the profile of growth in the euro area in the second and third quarters of this year and, following this, a progressive return to ongoing moderate growth.

JEAN-CLAUDE TRICHET, 2008

I hoped to be enlightened by the economists. I also expected them to hold up their hands and admit they were wrong. Because the fact is most of the profession failed to predict the catastrophe that was coming. Some say it was impossible to predict. Nonsense! Not only was it predictable, but an economic science unable to make correct predictions is not very scientific, if at all.

GIOVANNI SARTORI, 2008

Why did nobody see this awful crisis coming?

QUEEN ELIZABETH II
speaking to economists at the London School of Economics in 2008.

It would be good if economists understood their subject better. Controlling debt and having solvent banks while making the economy grow is the magic formula people are looking for, so far without much success. Growth policies are desirable, but how do you fit them in with eradicating debt? Politicians and economists must find a solution, but it's not easy.

BILL GATES, 2012

Chapter 1

A Grave Crisis No Different From Any Other

The world is currently in the midst of an intense, profound economic crisis. The one key feature of economic growth between 1970 and 2010 (Figure 1.1) is that although the economy has expanded at times, there has been an overall downward trend. The curve has often followed the political climate and energy prices. For instance, the contractions in the 1970s were caused by the Yom Kippur War and the Arab Oil Embargo between October 1973 and March 1974. The consequences of these events and of Khomeini's Iranian Revolution drove the price of Brent crude oil up to $39.50 a barrel by 1980. Some years, worldwide growth almost reached zero, and growth clearly dwindled between 1979 and 1982. The economy began to expand again when energy prices fell to $11 in 1985 (an event closely related to the renewed growth), and the price of oil rose to $40.15 per barrel in September 1991, driven up by the First Gulf War. Global GDP plummeted once again during the war, but not to the extent that growth was negative. Since then, the global economy has gradually been slowing down, but fluctuations in energy prices fail to provide a mechanical explanation for this behaviour. The price per barrel escalated from $24.86 in October 1996 to $34.59 in October 2000, then climbed to almost $52 in January 2007. In between were the Asian crises (1997–99), 9/11, the start of the Second Gulf War, the July 2006 conflict between Israel and Hezbollah and concurrent reductions in oil production by OPEC. Throughout this process the economy continued to fluctuate, despite which the price of energy was rising at rates above 3.5% a year. At the end of 2007, growth stood at more than 5%, and in July 2008 Brent crude oil reached a record price of $146.69, before dropping to $44.80 by February 2009. The Great Recession had begun to show its face and had a tangential relationship with these fluctuations. The aggregate global GDP data, which were positive, only served to hide disparate situations and the rise of new powers: the emerging countries, dominated by Asia. Though Figure 1.1 is intentionally concise, the underlying data reflect major economic dislocations, which I will try to explain.[1]

The crisis that began in 2007–8 has much in common with previous eras, and therefore some of its defining features were also present in the crises of yesteryear. But it is also true that the size and depth of the economic downturns throughout the developed world pose new challenges to economics and to cabinet members who design and implement economic policies. Important lessons were learned from the 1929 Wall Street Crash and the social and economic developments that followed, thanks to which the mistakes of that era were never made again. But now new game-changing events have emerged from the drama of a crisis that, from today's perspective,

Figure 1.1 Global GDP Growth, 1970–2010

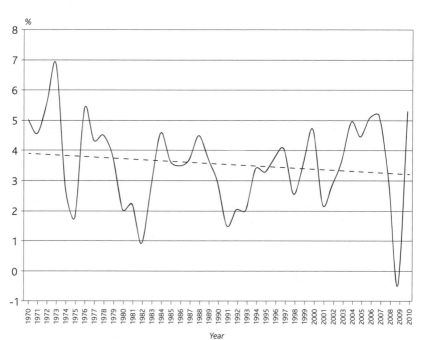

Source: By the author, based on IMF data.

shows contradictory signs resulting from intense, extensive volatility and from the current revival of all the precepts of neo-liberal economics.

American economic policy since the 1980s has given rise to a new vision and approach that have come from academia, especially Harvard University and Martin Feldstein. In the most conservative economic circles, this former advisor to President Reagan is seen as the successor to Milton Friedman, the University of Chicago economist who created the Chicago School, a school of thought that in practice has had a dismal track record. Feldstein's most prominent disciples, whose doctoral theses he supervised, were given lofty positions in the George H.W. Bush administration. The crux of his argument is simple and blunt. He believes capital should be tax-free so it will generate enough savings for private investment to stimulate strong economic growth and better productivity while eliminating inflation. This school gives little thought to work and, needless to say, workers. Intellectuals, so often lacking in imagination, have called this ancient and failed recipe neo-economics, a term reminiscent of neo-liberalism, to which it is closely attached. But this theoretical short-sightedness reminds economic historians of the generic characteristics of the Victorian economy (from the second half of the 19th century to the start of World War I), so the prefix "neo" is a bit of a joke. We are faced, therefore, with a new commodity that has already produced vast rivers of ink and will make quite a few people wealthy. But let us look at the main objectives of this so-called neo-economics as it applies to areas of the public economy in the US.[2]

First, its supporters want to upend the tax system completely and move it in a firm direction: reducing the tax burden on investment income and maintaining it on income from work. They want a flat tax rate in order to gradually abolish public-sector involvement in social services, health and education. They have thus reduced the gap between the top tax rate and the next one down, eliminated double taxation on dividends as well as inheritance tax and transfer tax, and made it easier to defer tax on capital goods. Moreover, now that the accounts do not add up, a tangible proposal to cut the imbalances is being put on the table for discussion: privatization. This shift in direction, welcomed with open arms by most European governments, is of major importance. It is not about placing public companies on the market – which nearly all governments have done, with varying success – but about privatizing strategic social services that form the core of the welfare state: health and pensions. Furthermore, this is related to the shift towards more regressive fiscal policies: instead of top earners paying the most tax, indirect taxes mean that rich people pay less to the treasury, supposedly because they will invest more and create more wealth. As I have pointed out, right-wing parties in Europe pay close attention to this economic philosophy and have no qualms about implementing it. They talk about "cutting back the size of the state" as the key to tackling the economic problems of competitiveness and productivity. It is total hypocrisy, because the most fervent advocates of this so-called ultraliberal orthodoxy are usually the very same people and organizations that drink copiously from the wells of public funds and who are "bailed out" when tough times come along, without later being forced to give anything in return. The recent problems with the financial system are the most illustrative example of this. Thus, the private sector blends in with the public sector like a chameleon, exchanging sundry lucrative financial transactions that benefit certain business leaders and companies and condition the policies of underdeveloped countries hoping to find their own place in the global economy. It is nothing short of a fraud, as John Kenneth Galbraith has already made clear.[3] Those who champion the market also happen to have lucrative business deals with different levels of government, no matter who is in power. They depend on government and influence its decisions. It's not the market that works; it's contacts and influence. Examples abound everywhere. It seems this new stage of capitalism is ushering in the privatization of key, genuine policies that everyone can understand, such as welfare (education, health, social infrastructure), while there is a convergence between certain economic players and governments in areas that have huge potential to provide private profits, such as construction, conventional energy and the military industry. In this powerful ideological line the purest patriarchs are the new conservatives.

The secondary objective for supporters of neo-economics is to expand public spending. The tax cuts in the final years of the last conservative era in the US – the epicentre of the neo-economics movement – were concurrent with a government-spending hike of just over 8% per year, mainly on the military and security, bringing spending to its highest level since the 1960s. This issue is critical: the economic policy stimulated public debt, which according to the Congressional Budget Office deepened from 59.8% of GDP in 2001 to 65.3% in 2004, while the current account deficit rose from 3.9% to 5.1% during the same period. The figures have two worrying implications. First, the types of legislation being imposed on other parts of the world are not being considered in the United States (nor, importantly, in Germany or France, whose debt-to-GDP ratio is much higher than that of some of the countries under constant attack by speculators). In other words, America is unabashedly spending more than it is taking in, whatever measure you use. And second, these imbalances are paid for by the rest of the world: The US already exports little capital and needs inflows from countries like China, which is buying Wall Street bonds and American debt. This contributes to the weak dollar, with Washington's full complicity, despite the problems this spawns for the European export economies.

So, "Is neo-economics working?" From a social standpoint clearly it is not. One need only look at a few indicators drawn from public institutions in the US. During George W. Bush's final term of office the number of poor people in the world's biggest economy grew to almost 36.3 million, or 13% of the population. Meanwhile, there were about 44 million people without health care – just over 15% of the population – and this figure was falling at an ever-faster rate. Neo-economics makes the rich richer and widens the big salary differences in American society, while it also feeds massive imbalances that create huge uncertainties in the global markets.

However, many people in academia, the media and politics were quick to give a biased interpretation of how the situation came about. Using economics for political gain, many exaggerated the initial core of the crisis, reporting signs of a slowdown in economic growth as clear inklings of an impending economic crisis. Those who unwaveringly promulgated these ideas knew full well, thanks to data made public by trustworthy institutions, that there was no crisis back then, not even a hint of one. In fact, during this period, between August 2007 and the start of the summer of 2008, all developed countries had positive macroeconomic variables, and economic forecasters also said the outlook was positive.[4] In short, economic activity was clearly in decline, but the indicators were still positive and econometric models emphasized that an economic recovery was possible. In the main publications devoted to analysing the global economy for a general readership (*The Economist*, the *Financial Times*, *The Wall Street Journal*), neither the editorials nor the lead columnists were sounding the same warnings that some political oppositions were beginning to use to attack their governments. Despite the signs of an economic slowdown throughout the developed world, no economist belonging to the International Monetary Fund (IMF), the World Bank or the European Central Bank (ECB) nor any research services of major, respected financial institutions were talking about a crisis. Not in the strictest, most technical, most crucial and most dramatic sense of the word. Nearly all of us got it wrong.[5]

The reality, however, is that the initial economic policies used to tackle the recession resulted in spiralling debt and a wider deficit, and these spread to all the world's economies. Greece's deep financial difficulties were a warning that it might be difficult to repay government debt. Things got worse, because German and French banks were the ones involved in this predictable financial chaos. Then in spring 2010, Ecofin decided to adopt very stringent measures that ended up undermining the economic policies prescribed by the IMF and the World Bank just eight months earlier. The law of the pendulum acted ruthlessly, with the Greek crisis oozing a series of deliberate but false messages on the state of the Spanish economy, which was relegated to the same division as the Greek, Irish and Portuguese economies. The strategy of speculation was in motion: these signals served only to increase the cost of government borrowing in the south, thus benefiting the direct aggressors of those countries' economies.

The "markets" – a euphemism – are thus used to justify a host of corrective measures that some proposed roadmaps promote as ways to redress government finances. This has one particular corollary: it minimizes the time needed to implement these measures, so the deficit is expected to return below the threshold set in the Maastricht Treaty (3% of GDP), which means government debt has to be reduced urgently. Although economies were on the brink of a recovery that everybody had been announcing, with economic policies gradually but tangibly beginning to work, governments passed from an openly Keynesian approach to full-blown Chicago-school monetarist orthodoxy. Those nations with a debt-to-GDP ratio above 60% and a deficit above 3% of GDP had to produce recovery plans to restore market confidence – in markets which, paradoxically, were saved by government policies that shook the very indicators that were being criticized.

These rules of play were set by the European Central Bank, Deutsche Bank and Chancellor Angela Merkel. David Cameron's triumph in Britain underlined a clear alignment of these more severe government economic policies, and Cameron won even though the previous prime minister, Gordon Brown, literally saved the British financial system with a generous injection of public capital. Meanwhile, the other major European power, Nicolas Sarkozy, deliberately remained non-committal in a way not seen on the other side of the Atlantic, where President Obama and his economic team decided to continue pursuing more Keynesian stimulus policies and look to redress the national deficit in the more distant future than in Europe. The American administration's ability to finance the economy through massive borrowing from China undoubtedly made this decision easier. But the decision has fuelled a heated debate in the economics departments of American universities and has shaken the consciences of leading experts – experts whose opinions are rarely called into question. This has been conveyed clearly in the media.[6] In fact, economists like Amartya Sen, Paul Samuelson, Paul Krugman, Joseph E. Stiglitz and Daniel McFadden, all Nobel laureates in economics, to name just a few (an exhaustive list would contain countless names and press references), wrote in the press about irrational consumers and investors, the need to create alliances between governments and markets, the criticism levelled at talk of a recovery, and the necessity to persevere with measures to stimulate the economy. Official postulates, meanwhile, essentially argued only in terms of balancing budgets at all costs (economic orthodoxy), reducing deficits and controlling prices. This dominant, permanent discourse has become the only way of thinking.[7]

Economic developments are highly erratic, with lightning-quick changes happening every day, even too quickly for economic and social operators, governments and the mysterious markets. It is getting more and more difficult to apply specific formulas based on one ideology of economics or another (fiscal consolidation vs. more interventionist strategies). Various European elections have been marked by a series of promises on tax cuts, protecting the welfare state and stimulating investment that have not materialized once the party – of whatever colour – came to power. Those who promised, as a liberal article of faith, that the tax burden stymied economic recovery, that there would be no cuts to health, education and social services, and that there would be lax policies for entrepreneurs, opted to backpedal on all these plans once they took office. Stubborn, imperturbable reality overtook the vote-seeking campaign promises. The erratic nature of economic dynamics imposes a need for greater prudence in setting economic agendas, and makes the useless dogmas less appealing. Crises lead to crossroads, to new challenges, but also to all kinds of depressions. Creative destructions emerge from these upheavals if they are accompanied by effective synergies between the public and private sectors. This is as true for small, regional, limited economies as it is for much larger, more robust ones.

This is why the word "subversive" is used in the title of this book. To subvert means to disrupt, destroy, stir things up, especially morally. It means to change the established order and assumptions. The concept of subversion usually has negative connotations, with many aspects related to depraved deviations from the status quo. But in times such as these, perhaps it is more innovative and refreshing to propose subversive ideas than to maintain current, conventional, orthodox trends. I believe this might even help build a more democratic culture in which citizens express individual, subjective opinions and question (and change) them if they find new, more convincing arguments. As Albert O. Hirschman argued, at some point in life self-subversion can actually become the very core of self-renewal. Existentialism and science come together in this seemingly contradictory axiom. This idea is a powerful reminder of the process described by Joseph Schumpeter, when he attributed an innovative force to certain entrepreneurs – not to all of them, but to those with the conviction and capacity to subvert the known conditions for production and distribution and thus to break the rules of the game and create new ones. It is also a reminder of the words of the Nobel literature laureate Hermann Hesse when, speaking through his protagonists (whether Demian or Steppenwolf), he says that whoever wants to be born again must destroy a world.

Hirschman's refers to the simple yet powerful notions of "exit" and "voice". By "exit" he means the act of withdrawing, of leaving places you don't like, silently or audibly; by "voice" he means voicing a complaint, launching a protest, perhaps after having "exited" (and this is crucial) to achieve the quality that has been damaged. The reflection is an appropriate response to discourses that reinforce a single, uncritical, rigid way of thinking, beyond which there is nothing but absolute vacuity and inaction. The "reformers" (a euphemism for "destroyers of hard-won social benefits" that have been sacrificed on the altar of the markets) would do well to draw a diagram of the damage their proposals might inflict upon some of society's other values. Trying to stimulate economic growth while reducing the social inequalities the growth will cause can require very divergent policies depending on what part of the economy is growing, or in the technical jargon, what the real composition of GDP is. The same can happen if you aim to cut the deficit while maintaining social services: it is as impossible as squaring the circle, as paradoxical as a fractal without repeating patterns. The problem is finding a combination of policies that do as little damage as possible to either objective, knowing that often it is impossible to do both of these well, as evidenced by the real economy, which the supporters of rigid economic models insist on misrepresenting.

The honest thing to do, from an intellectual standpoint and in terms of practical applications, would be to acknowledge that finding something resembling an optimal solution will be more likely if we admit we are faced with competing, conflicting objectives. Or, more concisely, imbalances. Denying such evidence will steer economic policy towards an unwelcome scenario of inefficiency: a scenario of deceit, of blatant lies hidden behind vague generalizations (usually the great breeding ground for falsehood) and simple and abstract ideas — all for electoral, professional and political gain. As Bertolt Brecht says, hidden behind these postulates are those who, like parrots, repeat general ideas and complaints with no desire to be more specific. I can think of a few: they refer incessantly to the free market, legal certainty, support for entrepreneurs, lower taxes, etc., all of these dressed in robes of freedom. Even so, Brecht points out that as a group, they do so in a way that ensures they continue to receive what they consider their fair share of the spoils. So basically they only admit one truth: that which suits them.[8]

Notes

1. The oil-prices data at http://www.wtrg.com cover from 1869 to 2011.
2. Those with a poor conceptual framework very often wind up using terms that conflate similar behaviours. Thus there is a characteristic shared by "neo-economics", "neo-conservatism" and "neo-liberalism": an ideological consensus on macroeconomic management that covers public policy and extends to the most microeconomic levels. Behind these supposedly technical ideas is a firm political response designed to discipline and reactivate practices more closely related to the gold-standard economy and society. In this respect, the class view – the purely social approach to the conflict – is openly put forward as a control tool whose most direct, immediate and profound manifestation is found in austerity measures. See D. Harvey, *A Brief History of Neoliberalism* (Oxford: Oxford University Press, 2007); J. Ziegler, *L'Empire de la Honte* (Paris: Fayard, 2005). A more general overview, though from a similar standpoint, is J.A. Frieden, *Global Capitalism: Its Fall and Rise in the Twentieth Century* (New York: W.W. Norton, 2006).
3. J.K. Galbraith, *The Economics of Innocent Fraud: Truth for our Time* (London: Penguin Books, 2004). Thus, for instance, the policies of "kicking away the ladder", as the great 19th-century economist Friedrich List put it, is another key form of action for developed countries, who preach economic liberalism but do not practice it in the slightest in their international relations. This creates a blockade preventing goods produced by underdeveloped countries from entering the market more freely and penalizes their protectionist policies aimed at stimulating their emerging production sectors. See H. Chang, *Kicking Away the Ladder. Development Strategy in Historical Perspective* (London: Anthem, 2002); E. Reinert, *How Rich Countries Got Rich . . . and Why Poor Countries Stay Poor* (London: Constable, 2007); and the classic F. List, *National System of Political Economy* (London: Longmans & Co., 1904).
4. The figures consulted in the IMF, OECD and European Commission databases for those years were all positive. Constant revisions to the figures led to a negative outlook for some countries in 2009 and 2010, with forecasts that proved erratic.
5. I say "nearly all of us" for obvious reasons. The great Italian economist Paolo Sylos Labini deserves due credit. He warned that the increase in public and private debt in America would be unsustainable and would lead to a global crisis (Paolo Sylos Labini, "Le prospettive dell'economia mondiale", *Moneta e Credito*, 223 (September 2003)). This work has been widely praised by the Italian post-Keynesian school, particularly by Alessandro Roncaglia in *Economisti che sbagliano* (Bari: Laterza, 2010) and *Il mito della mano invisibile* (Rome: Laterza, 2005).

6. Alan Greenspan, the all-powerful Chairman of the Federal Reserve when the crisis broke out in earnest, admitted to making mistakes in his perceptions of the economic situation, having been completely absorbed by the exuberance of stock movements and the foolish attitudes of the banking sector. Greenspan's decision to set interest rates that turned negative in real terms between 2002 and 2005 expanded the availability of credit, which was spurred on by the financial engineering of derivatives (see Greenspan's self-critical remarks in *The Wall Street Journal*, 24 October 2008).

7. Krugman, without doubt one of the most influential economists in the media, discusses the lethal consequences of Greenspan's and the US administrations' policies in the article "Revenge of the Glut". He vehemently defends public investment, quoting Romer and Bergstein, who said that "a dollar of infrastructure spending is more effective in creating jobs than a dollar of tax cuts". He also calls for profound reforms to the financial system, and believes that a couple of years in the red should not be an obstacle to intensive demand policies, arguing that "spending money now means a stronger economy, both in the short run and in the long run." See selected opinion articles published by Paul Krugman at the height of the crisis in *The New York Times* on 27 November 2008 ("Lest We Forget"), 11 January 2009 ("Ideas for Obama"), 1 February 2009 ("Bailouts for Bunglers"), 1 March 2009 ("Revenge of the Glut"), 28 May 2009 ("The Big Inflation Scare"), 2 July 2009 ("That '30s Show"), 20 September 2009 ("Reform or Bust"), 2 October 2009 ("Mission Not Accomplished"), 18 October 2009 ("The Banks Are Not All Right"), and 1 November 2009 ("Too Little of a Good Thing"). Particularly interesting is the article "How Did Economists Get It So Wrong", published on 6 September 2009.

8. See A.O. Hirschman, *A Propensity to Self-Subversion* (Cambridge, MA: Harvard University Press, 1995); J.A. Schumpeter, *Can Capitalism Survive? Creative Destruction and the Future of the Global Economy* (New York: HarperPerennial, 2009); B. Brecht, *Writing the Truth: Five Difficulties* (New York: Grove Press, 1966). Robert E. Lane has questioned whether the market can make people happy, even saying speculators may act aggressively because of their internal unhappiness, which they try to escape from by succeeding in finance. See R.E. Lane, *The Market Experience* (Cambridge: Cambridge University Press, 1991); A.O. Hirschman, *A Propensity to Self-Subversion*.

Chapter 2

A Systemic Crisis in the Context of Globalization

1. America in recession

"New" globalization, as opposed to "old" globalization (which some economic historians place in the late 19th century) is producing a plethora of literature aiming to explain, from different standpoints, how capitalism works at what is considered to be a time of readjustment.[1] Various slants have been looked at, with the most observant analysts seeing the emergence of possible new economic drivers that will come to the fore. This is the direction taken by the most recent academic works on the vast Asian region, which look at how production systems, education and cultural elements affect growth patterns. In short, these works predict that Asian countries will go on to dominate the global economy, leading to industry relocations and short-term crises.[2]

There is also a mountain of literature on the economics of China, underlining the progress made by the ancient Cathay area over the last twenty years. This progress is occurring at vastly different speeds: crisis-ridden regions and sectors and archaic equipment coexist with dynamic regions and industries that are using modern technology. Although authors agree that official Chinese figures are unreliable, China is still growing much more quickly than other developing countries and has consistently been closing the gap to richer countries. The compound datum given shows that China has been ranked among the top three global exporters since 2000 thanks in part to its capacity to attract foreign capital and companies seeking to reduce their wage bill and environmental costs. In this new phase of globalization, dominated by business relocations and firm commitments to the latest technologies, the imposing Chinese colossus has become the "world's workshop", as Françoise Lemoine put it, a description that reminds us of the pioneering British industrial revolution.[3]

In this context, it is interesting to consider the leading role to be played by America, which despite the restructuring of the global economy remains the world's biggest power. The more orthodox academic contributions emphasize the potentialities of American government policies, especially under Republican administrations, which deregulate the economy and financial system in a misconceived sense of the "invisible hand" of the markets. These authors overlook the massive deficits under the presidencies of Ronald Reagan and the two Bushes simply because they were not a result of benefits provided to those most in need or by government investment in health and education, but by lavish tax cuts for top earners – using the flawed Laffer curve as an alibi – and increased spending on the American military complex, with clear if indirect connections between political and economic power. Other academic authors, however, reject these arguments from an economic history and economics standpoint.[4]

Robert Brenner has published game-changing research on the shift from feudalism to capitalism. The vastly experienced economic historian has come to blows with Neo-Smithian Marxism embodied first by Paul Sweezy then by Immanuel Wallerstein. He has also written an extraordinary book on 17th-century English tradesmen and has shed interesting light on the current crisis.[5] Brenner's approach is clear: the world economy has failed to overcome the long decline that began with the 1973 crisis, so for him the outlook is gloomy. Excess capacity in global industry is the main economic cause of the situation, and the eruption of new technologies made the situation worse. Business profitability, he argues, declined greatly (by around 20% between 1997 and the turn of the century in non-financial activities) because of over-investment that fed this huge speculative bubble in stock market movements. This process has been aided by the main economic institutions, particularly the Federal Reserve, which gave incorrect signals to the markets and has fed this disproportionate investment. This led to the collapse of some sectors of the economy, including telecommunications. According to Brenner, who cites other experts' contributions to theories on excess capital accumulation, these are the foundations of the current recession. This theory has been circulated at other times from historical, economic and sociological perspectives by Samir Amin, Hosea Jaffe and André Gunder Frank, who adapted the Kondratieff waves of technological change.[6] More recently, Immanuel Wallerstein blamed the US's reduced capacity since the early 1970s on the rise of Japan and Europe and claimed we were witnessing the decline of American dominance. In an intelligent, well-documented work, the French historian Emmanuel Todd likened US expansion to that of Ancient Rome as the Empire began to crumble. He found new patterns in the fall of empires, including the massive cost of maintaining them and the drain on public finances. So according to Brenner, Wallerstein and Todd, we are witnessing a grave systemic crisis led by a weakened United States, which now has more consumers than producers and is seeing new protest movements within the country whose calls are quite different from those of the more conventional political left.[7] This recession is bringing about a productive transformation that is redefining the "centre" and the "periphery", to use Wallerstein's terminology. Other countries are being called to the economic fore – not the military fore – of globalization.[8]

The most direct source of the crisis began in 2000, resulting in a marked loss in profits.[9] Excess production capacity drove down prices, bursting the first stock-market bubble, the dot-com bubble. The bubble was fuelled by deregulation of the financial markets and the search for investment funds by companies that were losing profitability. The situation was made possible by the disinformation provided by top executives, who were paid with stock options based on dwindling profits. In 2000, telecommunications, which accounted for 3% of US GDP, had a stock portfolio worth 2.7 trillion dollars, or 15% of non-financial corporations in the United States, but still needed funding. The amount of funding grew by 15% a year between 1996 and 2000.

This process led to more than 300,000 new jobs, resulting in economic patterns similar to those seen in other technology sectors, which had similar opportunities at obtaining cheap capitalization. The Nasdaq index shot up at an astonishing rate, higher than that achieved by the Dow Jones, thus inflating a bubble fed by links with the real economy: household debt and higher imports. There was thus a chain of knock-on effects: higher demand was aided by a strong dollar that encouraged purchases from abroad, notably high-tech components from Asia, especially Japan, and cars, machines and other products from Europe, benefiting Germany and Italy in particular. The more this model set in, the wider the trade deficit became, with the US buying more than it sold and spending more than it earned. The result: a clear deficit scenario caused by various related factors, so it would be short-sighted to act on only one of those elements, as the Federal Reserve did by cutting interest rates. The path towards the Great Recession of 2007–8 was being laid out.[10]

Against this backdrop, the outbreak of corporate scandals was just the tip of an iceberg immersed in a sea of opacity. Over-investment in technology sectors generated by completely asymmetric information (on this point see Joseph Stiglitz's groundbreaking academic contributions)[11] led to bankruptcies in the telecommunications sector and left more than half a million people jobless. Excess production capacity gave rise to excess supply that the market was unable to absorb. The data provided by Brenner say it all: annual growth in investment plummeted from 12.5% to 0.1% in 2000, then shrank by 5.2% in 2001 and 3% in 2002, while exports stagnated. Wider deficits, aggravated by less attractive US assets, put pressure on the dollar and weakened it against the euro. Foreign direct investment into the US fell by 60% in 2001, while purchases of American shares fell by more than 35% in the same year. Despite the weaker dollar, the trade balance didn't recover, with the Asian markets and Canada continuing to feed the consumer society in the US, while the European economy was contracting and beginning to experience bigger blows due to the drop in American demand.

Stiglitz complements Brenner's perspective, although he mounts a vehement defence of Clinton's economic policy, especially the big reduction in the pre-existing deficit and the tangible concern for social problems and environmental externalities. The latter led to heavy investment in updating facilities in the public and private sectors, a marked increase in productivity (Brenner also highlights this), new jobs and control of inflation. So despite the many points shared by Brenner and Stiglitz, the latter has a much less pessimistic view of how the American economy evolves. However, Jeff Madrick has said that, unlike in the past, this boom in the American economy was not accompanied by major productivity improvements. According to his data, growth averaged 2.85% for 1947–73 and 1% for 1973–2000, so it was much lower during the period in which production processes and services were being computerized. This has led some to believe that perhaps this is a technologically advanced era with a small-scale economy based on the skills, knowledge and ingenuity of workers and small-business owners, rather than on the strength of big companies and chains of distribution. As you will gather, this is a highly contentious issue. While there are signs that US productivity growth is accelerating thanks to what has been dubbed the "new economy", some authors such as Paul Krugman are sceptical, questioning the method used to calculate the productivity of the services sector, which is much more volatile than manufacturing.[12]

Madrick's figures do not differ much from those of Manuel Castells, who is convinced that the world economy played a vital role in increasing productivity.[13] But despite these criticisms, Stiglitz offers a mosaic of major indicators regarding Clinton's presidency, which summarizes a virtuous process: strong growth, without major price changes, control of the deficit and more employment. Unemployment was as low as 3.9% in 2000, without inflationary spikes, and according to Stiglitz this reduced poverty and dramatically reduced crime. Nevertheless, he is self-critical, saying that focusing the economy on finances, the deficit and inflation meant putting aside commitments to poorer parts of the population and to the environment. It is those commitments, according to Stiglitz, that distinguish Democratic Keynesianism from Republican Keynesianism, which throws all its investment into the military.

Nevertheless, despite the different interpretations in economics literature, there is a certain consensus regarding the causes of the crisis:

(A) The irrational exuberance of the stock market bubble. Stiglitz puts it bluntly, saying that asset prices were completely independent of their underlying values. Billions of dollars were poured into profit-less companies, which then requested additional funding by trading in the securities market. This was all made possible by creative accounting: basically falsifying accounting entries. Companies considered to be completely solvent were pilloried when this came to light. Economic agents and political leaders were left in a state of disbelief, distrust and panic. Consortia such as Enron, Global Crossing, Qwest, World.com, Merck, Xerox, and Vivendi, along with financial institutions such as JP Morgan Chase and Merrill Lynch and auditing firms belonging to the Arthur Andersen group, all took a knock, to varying degrees, because of the white-collar theft of some of their executives. The guilty executives advised buying still more shares in their companies so they could make further investments; but they did quite the opposite, selling assets to inflate their own bank balances in a way never seen before. As Charles Kindleberger has shown, economic history is littered with events similar to those that have happened either side of the new millennium. But clearly few lessons have been learned.[14]

(B) The Federal Reserve's misguided policy. Alan Greenspan is part of the unleashing of Wall Street. That was the conclusion shared by authors like Brenner, Stiglitz and Krugman. Bob Woodward, the famous journalist who wrote a panegyric praising former Reserve chairman Greenspan, talks of Greenspan's euphoria in front of the computer screens watching the variables fit together in a veritable "virtuous circle" – as the head of US monetary policy put it – that imbued the lower inflation, unemployment and deficit and the higher productivity. The Federal Reserve gave enormous importance to the financial markets, continuing in its fascination with bolstering stock prices despite clear signs of the growing deficit. Greenspan offered his unequivocal support for George W. Bush's tax cuts. This policy clearly benefited the most powerful sectors of society, making the bubble even fatter. There was vitriolic criticism of this strategy. The Chairman of the Federal Reserve became embroiled as an accomplice in crucial aspects of fiscal policy rather than acting more moderately and focusing more strictly on monetary policy.

(C) The proliferation of asymmetric information. Brenner and Stiglitz conclude that the "invisible hand" referred to by Smith does not exist. Instead, they adopt a position similar to that developed by the Nobel laureate Kenneth Arrow in collaboration with Gérard Debreu, in that a series of conditions must be set for the market to be balanced and to work without outside interference.[15] One of those requirements is for perfect information, which companies can then use to forecast how their goods and services, and therefore their factors of production, will evolve. Stiglitz has investigated what happens when these conditions are not met, i.e. when the information is imperfect and asymmetrical, when not everyone has the necessary data to make rational choices. He reaches a stark conclusion: that even in the most developed countries the markets function differently from what the perfect-market theories predict. In fact, the terrible decisions seen at the microeconomic level are the result of disinformation given by many people involved in finance, including, albeit to a lesser extent, the Federal Reserve. It is difficult to make correct decisions when the information is asymmetrical and the main guardians of economic orthodoxy steer clear of major commitments and get caught up in the speculative wave.[16]

(D) The government's negligible role in providing balance. The economic downturn is attributed to the lack of government action. The totemic view of a deregulated market has brought about apathy in government in highly speculative areas. The most illustrative example was the cut in capital-gains tax in the US, a crucial issue that has showcased to the entire population how wealth can be generated quickly without tax constraints. In other words, those who make big profits on the stock markets end up paying less tax, which in turn encourages even bigger investment in stock-market assets, further inflating the bubble. Stiglitz argues that it would have been more beneficial to invest in education, infrastructure and R&D programmes to provide a more solid foundation for the improved productivity. This is a contentious issue, because the undeniable macroeconomic advances are distorted by the illusory phenomena of the stock market, which all economists are seduced by. It's a pity that Kindleberger's shadow was not cast more intensely on President Clinton's economic advisers. On this point, Stiglitz says principles were put to one side and skewed visions of reality were adopted, fuelled by the success of large macroeconomic aggregates. Two centuries of experience (economic history, again) of the problems caused by conflicts of interest and data that are neither homogeneous nor available to all economic stakeholders were disregarded.

(E) The obsessions with deficits and inflation. Reducing the deficit does not always solve economic downturns in the short term, and can even harm growth. Authors such as Brenner, Stiglitz and Krugman believe government should give more slack when dealing with deficits – except trade deficits – in certain carefully selected areas, especially technology projects, education, infrastructure and R&D initiatives. In other words, they believe governments should stimulate an economy with a high added value. Higher debt would increase corporate assets, so reducing the deficit would reduce those assets and make the country poorer. The symbiosis between economic policy and fiscal strategy is obvious: if the yields on investment are higher than the low interest rates on government borrowing, taxes on the rest of the economy can be cut. If these premises were applied to European economies, the economic roadmap would be very different. If governments' ability to borrow were severely limited in favour of an investment policy like the one described above, it would have a negative effect on any possible productivity gains. Furthermore, a monetary policy based on inflation is bad news in economies that have come dangerously close to having negative inflation, like America and certain European powers.[17] The Federal Reserve has acted with greater conviction to prevent this, acting resolutely to lower interest rates (although it acted less rationally towards the end of Greenspan's reign). The situation was different at the European Central Bank, which was dominated by over-rigid orthodoxy and unnuanced approaches, such as carefully monitoring price developments without considering the possible levers for economic growth. The economic "fat" that is gained when inflation rises above a certain level is not negative for economies that need sure-fire boosts to their jobs market and to education, technology and research.

Having looked at these causes, which on their own already suggest fairly clearly that there was oversaturation and too much volatility on the stock markets (although this is easy to see in hindsight, and much harder to spot when the process is starting out), let us now look at some essential indicators that highlight the imbalances that existed in the US:

• Office of Management and Budget figures for 2003 and 2004 showed fiscal deficits of more than $500 billion due to lower income and higher expenditure. This was caused by a "war budget" that promoted investment in security and defence and Bush's generous fiscal policy for those in the highest tax bracket.

• Department of Commerce data show that America's trade

deficit increased, despite the dollar weakening against the euro. Changes in the country's trade structure provide an explanation: Canada and the EU were America's main markets in 1995, but from 2003 the Chinese market exploded, and a year later trade barriers with Canada and Mexico were lifted thanks to the North American Free Trade Agreement. In these new trade areas, the US dollar remained a benchmark currency, so its price against the euro had little relevance.

- Office of Management and Budget figures show there were almost three million job losses between 2003 and 2005, revealing how the US jobs market was being chipped away at just over three years before the 2008 crisis burst onto the scene.

In short, the existing imbalances – which I have tried to summarize – combined with a dwindling jobs market are the difficult contrasts that question the most solid American macroeconomic data while establishing the foundations for the Great Recession.

2. Finances and the real economy: The outbreak of the 2008 crisis

Shortly before the summer of 2007, nobody was talking about a global economic crisis.[18] The data I have discussed above, which at the very least forewarned of a difficult economic situation, did not change people's perception of how the global economy would evolve. As in 1928 and a few months before October 1929, well-respected analysts, political experts, leading economists, consultancies, universities and politicians were stating categorically that the economy was healthy and the outlook was positive for the next few years. A plethora of literature has emerged on this topic, but some works deserve more attention than others, as many an opportunist has jumped on the economic prophecy bandwagon and claimed that he or she predicted everything, without saying where or when. We shouldn't pay much attention to these new gurus who, incredibly, are rather prominent in certain media.

The above suggests that the crisis could be detected in the crazy boom in technology stocks at the start of the new century, when dangerous seeds were being sown with the expansion of the derivatives markets and the over-permissiveness of the banks, which completely infected private debt and alarmingly threatened to transform it into government debt. But this is all based on hindsight, and was not obvious at the time. It's easy to say now that the bull has already run through the china shop and created all the damage. The economic slowdowns were not a major focus of concern for governments, but only for operators in close contact with the system for processing derivatives and their tempestuous inner workings, those who could see a bigger picture of what was happening and had the capacity to make the right decisions. Despite this, the government leaders who had accurate data on the financial situation unquestionably continued to trust in the very liberal axiom of giving the markets free rein to operate without any hindrance and to search for the optimal points and best fit between supply and demand. This is all very ideological, spurred on by a blind faith in deregulation that was flooding the fiat money markets without any real support.

In this respect, Michael Lewis believes two forms of conduct help explain the current banking crises:[19] greed and incompetence.[20] There are many examples of both. It was greed that led banks to issue sub-prime mortgages – loans to borrowers who were quite likely not to be able to repay them. One should bear in mind the following two facts:

1. As long as house prices continued to rise, the property would cover the value of the loan. Originators didn't record loans on their balance sheets because they would sell the loans on to Wall Street investment banks. The investment banks would then turn the loans into collateralized debt obligations, or CDOs. CDOs are a type of security backed by an institution's assets – in this case, mortgages. All this would form a kind of pyramid-shaped gear system (CDOs have various grades and are grouped according to the level of risk), with the summit being what rating agencies rate as AAA. CDOs were a lucrative product for many financial institutions, because they offered higher yields than other investment opportunities.

2. These products, which were already viewed with suspicion by some quarters from a business point of view, needed some kind of guarantee. Because the system was so sophisticated, another product needed creating – the credit default swap, or CDS – to insure a certain amount of capital. It is the equivalent of taking out insurance against a default. But like any financial products, a CDS can be used to cover risks, but also to take them on – in other words, to speculate. CDSs also have a feature that distinguishes them from other insurance products: they can be sold to third parties. The resulting scenario seems flawless: a CDS is taken out as protection against banks that are laden with CDOs (which are overvalued). Operations equivalent to investment funds, which specialize in investing in CDOs (which were formed by sub-prime mortgages), were formed too. However, this whole mesh of derivatives, which formally are very solid and boost market confidence, have one thing in common, given the catastrophic end I have already discussed. They are all fuelled by greed, incompetence, and repeated harmful actions, affecting society by raining ruin and misery on many sectors of the population. The only way to prevent these recurring crises is to step up government regulation of financial institutions.

But greed and incompetence were not the only causes of the crisis. They were accompanied by other factors, including speculation, over-indebtedness, new financial instruments that do not reduce risk, the dubious role of ratings agencies, the collapse of the control mechanisms imposed by financial market regulation, and ultimately, the lack of government intervention in these tumultuous circumstances. Government intervention is a crucial factor, and needs to be very different from how it was during the recessions that immediately preceded the current major crisis. Let's remind ourselves of what has happened:

(A) In reaction to the dot-com bust in 2000 and the uncertainty caused by 9/11, the Federal Reserve's monetary policy was very lax. This led to falling interest rates, which in turn sparked additional residential property demand, greater household and company debt, and higher property prices. The actions and approaches adopted by the chairman of the Federal Reserve were clearly based on the belief that economic cycles had disappeared. This belief comes from poorly conceived philosophies such as the end-of-history theory, which lavishes praise on neo-liberal economics. The Federal Reserve's actions infected the whole system. The ideology of economics meant the defeat of a process of economic growth that seemed unstoppable.

(B) The European Central Bank adopted a more moderate policy, but it was not enough to contain the speculative bubbles in countries like Spain and Ireland. The rise in interest rates in 2006 to cool the overheating economy pushed up mortgage prices just as oil prices had increased too. This had immediate consequences, with housing demand and prices dropping and arrears and defaults becoming more frequent. The economic picture was very different across Europe with big variations in the indicators (government debt, debt-to-GDP ratio, inflation, unemployment, growth prospects) and measures that were particularly harmful to countries on the periphery of the European Union, such as Spain, Portugal, Greece and Italy.

(C) Governments began to intervene in financial institutions they considered too big to fail under any circumstances. This notion, excellently analysed by Gary Stern and Ron Feldman,[21] was first applied in 1985 to save the major American bank Continental Illinois, but has been repeated by government so many times that powerful banks have embarked upon high-risk investments knowing full well the government won't leave them in the lurch and will make taxpayers foot the bill. It is these government moves to bail out troubled financial institutions that turn private debt into public debt, and this affects the solvency of many developed countries. This is nothing new. As far back as 2005 there were already worrying signs that America's sovereign debt was too high, and Carmen Reinhart and Kenneth Rogoff said that in the coming years this would increase the debt of the worst affected countries by around 80%.[22] One cannot neglect considering causes of the 2008 crisis from a more historical perspective. There were causes linked to crucial factors like industrial over-production and financial wealth, which reveal the excess savings in the world – liquidity that has no plausible route into the real economy and is therefore thrown into the financial markets.[23] This idea is salient in the works of Brenner and Stiglitz, and ties in with perspectives of classical economics.

A deeper analysis of the situation reveals the following:

1. Over-production has brought about huge trade imbalances and financial dysfunctions. In the United States and Europe, higher industrial productivity led to excess stocks that were not met by demand. At the same time, Western companies were offshoring even bigger parts of their production processes to emerging countries like China and India. This strategy brought wages down in developed countries and pushed up total industrial production. There was also a substantial shift in the area of trade, with the increased production flooding the more developed markets (in Europe and the US), bringing down prices and pushing up unemployment. This is a powerful reminder of the similar explanations given for what sparked off the 1929 crisis, when over-production and low consumption determined the depth of the recession in the real economy.

2. In the finance sector, capital began to flow from emerging to developed countries for the first time ever. Starting in the 1990s, loans from emerging countries and innovations in financial products helped significantly increase consumption in developed countries, even over and above their means. In developed countries, imports far outweighed exports, while current-account balances were plunging further and further into the red and balances of payments were becoming negative year after year (see Table 2.1 and Figure 2.1).

The data, which are for an important set of European countries, show Germany's economy powering forward while other economies are contracting. Germany's economic power is clearly manifest in its current-account balance as a percentage of GDP, which is positive for the periods 1971–78, 1982–90 and 2001–8. These figures, always positive, show the extent of Germany's export capacity and the strength of its services sector. It is important to note that when Germany adopted the euro it strengthened its position, sending the country's current-account balance to record levels while that of other countries fell below zero. The best example is France (the other European powerhouse): its balance had been positive from 1992 to 2004, but turned negative as the country became less competitive. The same happened in Italy, where the new industrial economy in the industrial districts boosted exports, giving the country positive balances between 1993 and 2000 before it joined the bulk of countries that repeatedly had negative balances. These data clearly, albeit

Table 2.1 Current-account balances as percentages of GDP

Year	Greece	France	Germany*	Portugal	Spain	UK	Italy
1970						1.6	0.7
1971			0			1.9	1.3
1972			0.1			0.3	1.4
1973			1.1			-1.3	-1.7
1974			2.1			-3.8	-4.3
1975		0.8	0.7	-4.1	-3.5	-1.5	-0.3
1976	-3.1	-0.9	0.7	-6.6	-4	-0.6	-1.3
1977	-3.1	-0.1	0.7	-4.7	-1.9	0.1	0.9
1978	-2.2	1.4	1.3	-2.1	0.8	0.7	2
1979	-3.6	0.8	-0.6	-0.2	0.4	-0.2	1.6
1980	-4	-0.6	-1.7	-3.4	-2.5	1.3	-2.3
1981	-4.8	-0.8	-0.7	-15.3	-2.7	2.8	-2.5
1982	-3.6	-2.1	0.7	-11.2	-2.4	1.6	-1.8
1983	-3.9	-0.9	0.6	-6.3	-1.8	1.1	0.2
1984	-4.6	-0.2	1.3	-2.6	1.1	0.4	-0.8
1985	-7.1	0	2.5	1.5	1.6	0.7	-0.9
1986	-3.1	0.3	3.9	3.1	1.6	-0.2	0.4
1987	-1.9	-0.5	3.6	0.9	-0.1	-1.8	-0.3
1988	-1.3	-0.5	4	-2	-1	-4.2	-0.8
1989	-3.4	-0.5	4.3	0.3	-2.7	-5.1	-1.4
1990	-3.8	-0.8	2.8	-0.2	-3.5	-3.9	-1.5
1991	-1.6	-0.5	-1.3	-0.8	-3.5	-1.8	-2
1992	-1.9	0.3	-1	-0.2	-3.5	-2.2	-2.3
1993	-0.7	0.7	-0.9	0.3	-1.1	-1.8	0.8
1994	-0.1	0.5	-1.4	-2.3	-1.2	-1	1.3
1995	-2.2	0.7	-1.1	-0.1	-0.3	-1.2	2.2
1996	-3.3	1.3	-0.5	-4.2	-0.4	-0.9	3.2
1997	-3.6	2.7	-0.4	-5.9	-0.1	-0.1	2.7
1998		2.6	-0.6	-7.1	-1.2	-0.4	1.6
1999	-5.4	3.1	-1.3	-8.5	-2.9	-2.4	0.7
2000	-7.8	1.7	-1.7	-10.3	-4	-2.7	-0.5
2001	-7.2	2	0	-9.9	-4	-2.1	-0.1
2002	-6.5	1.4	2	-8.1	-3.2	-1.8	-0.8
2003	-6.6	0.8	1.9	-6.1	-3.5	-1.6	-1.3
2004	-5.9	0.6	4.7	-7.6	-5.3	-2.1	-1
2005	-7.4	-0.6	5.1	-9.5	-7.4	-2.6	-1.7
2006	-11	-0.7	6.5	-10	-9	-3.5	-2.6
2007	-14.2	-1.2	7.9	-9.5	-10.1	-2.8	-2.4
2008	-14.4	-1.9	6.7	-12.2	-9.6	-3.4	-3.4

Source: The data are given in current US dollars. Produced by the author based on figures from the IMF's Balance of Payments Statistics Yearbook and data files.

* Figures for 1990 and earlier are for West Germany.

Figure 2.1 Balance of Payments of Selected European Economies, 1970–2008

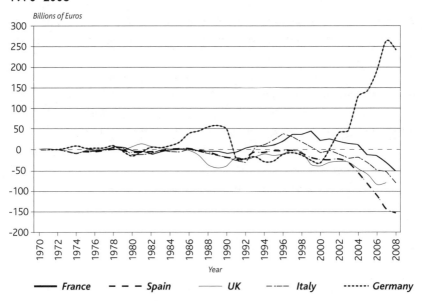

Billions of Euros

Source: Produced by the author based on IMF data, Balance of Payments Statistics Yearbook and data files.

superficially, illustrate the "two-speed economy" so often referred to by politicians and economists.[24]

The data in Figure 2.1 are even more powerful, because they refer to the full balance of payments, and they back up the observations made above: the curve for Germany rises way above all the others, while for France and Italy the curve begins to rise before falling away precisely when the single European currency is introduced. Figures 2.2 and 2.3 further confirm the hypothesis: the German economy takes off at the end of the 1990s and begins to soar at the start of the new century. The other countries, meanwhile, despite some variations, lose capacity and economic strength. Together, these data suggest that monetary union made the German economy even more dominant, contrary to what Eurosceptics say. They also suggest that the way the changeover to the single currency was designed gave Berlin the opportunity to shape the ECB's monetary policy. Given this context, it is hard to explain why highly orthodox economists

Figure 2.2 German Power: Trade and Services Balance

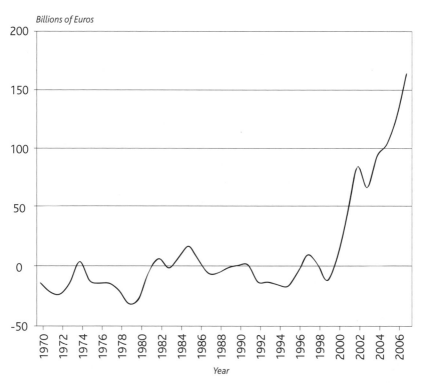

Billions of Euros

Year

Source: The data are given in current US dollars. Produced by the author, based on figures from the IMF's Balance of Payments Statistics Yearbook and data files.

tout German losses in the big European consortium and completely ignore how Germany has profited from its involvement in creating the economic structure, an event that now seems long ago given the complex transformations the European economy has been through since the turn of the century.

3. There are imbalances in international trade. Structural deficits set in while the US Federal Reserve was introducing expansive fiscal policies. The markets were at saturation point for goods and liquidity, leading to bubbles in asset prices. Governments were so passive, so entrenched in a distorted idea of *laissez-faire*, that they almost led the American economy to ruin, with immediate consequences for European economies. Since 1992, the United States had

Figure 2.3 European Decay: Trade and Services Balance

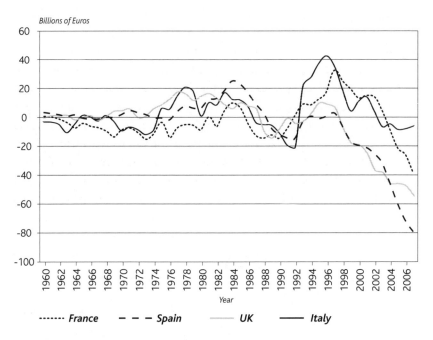

Source: The data are given in current US dollars. Produced by the author, based on figures from the IMF's Balance of Payments Statistics Yearbook and data files.

been consolidating its growing public and private demands, while the Japanese economy was beginning to stagnate and the EU was adapting its macroeconomy to the criteria set by the Maastricht Treaty. Emerging countries, meanwhile, were taking different steps. First, they were building up dollar reserves to protect them against financial instabilities (which were emerging as a result of the rampant deregulation promoted by those running Wall Street, with the blessing of the Federal Reserve). And second, the main oil producers in the Middle East were reducing crude oil supplies to the bare minimum to prevent a fall in oil prices. Meanwhile, countries with a trade surplus (China and Germany) were enlarging their economic capacity in order to invest in areas with a trade deficit. Finally, new World Trade Organization regulations forced emerging powers to introduce drastic changes to their exchange rates – mainly depreciations to continue helping exports to foreign markets. As exports grew, these countries were able to obtain new reserves, which they transferred to their aggregate savings, thus providing still more financial resources to the United States and other countries that were spending more than they could earn. This situation couldn't go on any longer, with the growth of the world's biggest economic power resting on a fragile foundation of cheap borrowing. The great paradox is that the world's last self-declared communist nation was and is providing the lion's share of the money borrowed by capitalism's superpower.

4. Financial panic erupted, driven by the opaque information and rumours regarding the reliability of derivatives, so the American, British and German governments came to the banks' rescue with huge cash injections that affected those countries' budgets. The central banks, meanwhile, cut interest rates, but this failed to make commercial banks, which were wary of each other's credit portfolios, open the credit taps. Stiglitz believes this had lethal consequences on the real economy: households were hurt by the drop in property prices; savings increased, driven by fear and uncertainty; credit became scarce, making the investment situation of businesses and families worse; and consequently, aggregate demand was blocked. The first quarter of 2008 thus saw the start of a poor economic cycle with very worrying results, including lower GDP and higher unemployment.[25]

5. According to reports published in early 2010 by reliable institutions, there was a high risk of the global economy entering recession towards the end of 2009. But experts still spoke of a positive outlook, albeit with certain poor indicators. The December 2009 edition of the *Consensus Forecast*, a monthly publication that pulls together the opinion of various institutions regarding the developments of the main economies, stressed how deviations from GDP growth forecasts for 2010 were, on average, 50% greater than normal. Table 2.2 shows a summary of data for the main institutions, with major errors in the forecasts. All of them show major errors for all countries, but the errors are greater for Germany. So the situation was anything but normal. And the risks being detected were related to the need to standardize fiscal and monetary policies, which would be the key to spurring a recovery. The authorities needed the accuracy of a brain surgeon: acting too quickly could stifle the stimuli, and acting too abruptly could weaken the recovery.

The precedents in economic history could not be more frightening. If governments want to avoid making the same mistakes, the policies adopted by Japan in the 1990s provide a perfect guide as to what not to do.[26] At the same time, drawing up a global plan for all countries presented a fundamental problem: not all countries' economies were in the same position, and there were major contextual differences between one country and another. A clear dilemma was presented to the Spanish finance ministry and treasury, and by extension to all governments: they could either pursue the policies labelled at that time as Keynesian, or return to more orthodox policies, dominated by specific aspects of economic monetarism. This was a clear reminder of the debate that took place in America between 1931 and 1933.[27]

The response was a return to a more orthodox economic policy based on observations of the data from Germany. In Europe's leading economy, gross fixed capital formation had fallen by well over 5% between the start of 2008 and around March or April of 2009 and exports had dropped by 12%, but the stimulus policies enabled by the laxity regarding the government deficit limits (which Merkel raised from 3% to 6% of GDP) put the German figures back in the black. Then, starting in May 2009, and particularly the last quarter of that year, Germany saw a marked recovery in investment and exports, which caused a rethink into the cold fiscal stimulus strategy that had been planned and that would affect all of Europe.[28]

At the same time, other EU countries were experiencing a similar recovery. The stimulus policies were clearly working, supporting investment and economic growth and helping reduce or ease unemployment. The only bad side was that they were pushing up government debts and deficits. These improvements were made despite dwindling private investment, prudence and caution in businesses, and a big upsurge in private savings, which was an unequivocal symptom of a drastic decline in consumer spending.

The financial crisis spread to markets that had invested heavily in American financial assets.[29] This contamination between economies also had ideological and methodological precedents. Those at the top

Table 2.2 Errors in economic forecasts

1. IMF

Forecast error before close of year (%)

	USA	Japan	Germany	France	Italy	UK	Spain
October 2008	1.6	1.9	0.8	0.7	1.2	1.1	0.5
October 2009	1.0	1.0	0.3	0.3	0.4	0.1	0.1
October 2010	−0.4	−1.2	−0.3	0.2	−0.3	0.3	−0.2

Forecast error one year earlier (%)

	USA	Japan	Germany	France	Italy	UK	Spain
October 2008	3.6	6.8		2.8	5.0	4.8	3.5
October 2009	−1.5	−2.3	−3.3	−0.3	−1.1	−0.5	−0.6

2. OECD

Forecast error before close of year (%)

	USA	Japan	Germany	France	Italy	UK	Greece	Portugal	Spain	Euro area
October 2009	1.0	1.0	0.2	0.3	0.3	−0.3	2.1	−0.3	0.1	0.2
October 2010	−0.3	−0.4	−0.1	0.2	−0.5	0.0	−0.4	0.1	−0.1	−0.1

Forecast error one year earlier (%)

	USA	Japan	Germany	France	Italy	UK	Greece	Portugal	Spain	Euro area
October 2009	−0.5	−2.3	−2.2	0.0	−0.4	−0.6	2.8	−0.6	−0.2	−0.9

3. European Commission

Forecast error before close of year (%)

	USA	Japan	Germany	France	Italy	UK	Greece	Portugal	Spain	Euro area
October 2009	1.0	0.4	0.1	0.5	0.4	−0.2	2.1	−0.4	0.0	0.2
October 2010	−0.3	−0.5	0.0	0.1	−0.4	0.0	−0.7	−0.1	−0.1	−0.2

Forecast error one year earlier (%)

	USA	Japan	Germany	France	Italy	UK	Greece	Portugal	Spain	Euro area
October 2009	−0.8	−2.9	−2.5	−0.3	−0.8	−0.9	3.2	−1.1	−0.7	−1.2

Source: By the author, based on IMF, OECD and European Commission data.

of the Wall Street hierarchy, prestigious universities, the most ultra-liberal political leaders and the Federal Reserve successfully lobbied for deregulation, and this deregulation soon became part of Britain's and Germany's financial fabric. British and German banks had amassed large amounts of US mortgage bonds, which is why the fall of Lehman Brothers affected the main groups in the financial system, which then tried to sell stock market assets at a time when pressure to sell was increasing by the hour. The assets lost value on the stock markets, resulting in widespread defaults. The Ponzi effects spread like wildfire, as predicted years earlier by Hyman Minsky, an economist who was as unknown at that time as he was quoted ad nauseam in the weeks after the economic bubbles burst.[30]

State interventionism was the order of the day in economic policy, with a clear plan: to save the financial system, whatever the cost, and thus prevent a domino effect and a chain of defaults not just of banks but also insurance companies closely involved with CDOs and CDSs.[31] Drastic measures have been taken to nationalize banks, such as in Britain, and masses of government money have been lavishly poured into banks by the US, Germany and France in astonishing events that have affected people's consciousness (the Keynesian "animal spirits"), as well as academic and political departments and experts around the world.[32] The situation, which people have come to believe is unprecedented, grossly shunning the lessons from economic history, casts doubt on ideals and premises that were thought to be untouchable: economic liberalism, the weight of civil society and the central doctrine of equilibrium in deregulated markets. There has even been some talk of re-engineering capitalism. Interest in Keynes has thus returned, and his old heated debates with Hayek, with their respective unwavering viewpoints, are being remembered again, although the initial, instinctive temptation is to follow the advice of Keynes. While Hayek blamed the 1929 crisis on inflation, caused by excess credit, which led to an unsustainable capital structure, Keynes believed it broke out because there was too little investment and demand was unable to match existing production. Robert Skidelsky draws a parallel between these postulates and the current crisis. He says Hayek's argument suggests the recession is due to lax monetary policy, which allowed banks to lend more money to businesses than the public could save on their current income. Therefore, "bad" investments were being financed by credit creation rather than by savings. This led to bubbles that fuelled a consumption boom, and when the whole thing collapsed the

American economy slumped. The parallel with Keynes is that recession begins when profit expectations fall relative to the amount being saved. When that happens, businesses prefer liquidity over investment. The obvious consequences are higher interest rates precisely when they need to be lower. So the crisis was caused by lack of investment rather than too much debt; high debt was a consequence of the recession, not a cause.[33]

The Keynesian arguments were gaining weight all the time. For instance, in its *World Economic Outlook* the IMF warned governments they needed to intervene in their banking systems using taxpayers' money to neutralize the effects of damaged, toxic assets. The report urged governments to do everything they could to prevent a repeat of the 1930 collapse. In the IMF's most important reports (*Global Financial Stability Report* and *World Economic Outlook*), it directly and indirectly defended government intervention in economic activity through public-spending increases to offset the decline in aggregate demand. As I have said, we were witnessing, albeit fleetingly, the return of Keynes.[34]

In this respect, there is one essential factor to be considered: that Germany has been one of the hardest-hit developed economies in the Great Recession, with GDP declining by more than 5%. In 2009, the German government reacted by cancelling the Stability and Growth Pact along with its EU partners and permitting eurozone countries to have a budget deficit of up to 6%, as we have already seen. But in 2010, when the global economy began to pick up and there was greater potential for German exports, Chancellor Merkel decided to return to the original Maastricht Treaty limit of 3%. Keynes had once again been expelled to the tomb of oblivion. The fiscal stimulus approach had been short-lived, and starting in May 2010 all governments began to adopt rigid economic conservatism in the form of rampant austerity programmes. Germany began to set its own terms, followed some way behind by France, forcing all countries to adopt tough austerity measures that are having terrible consequences for society. Thus the German giant does not act as a leader of the European economy but rather it establishes a more "nationalist" view of the economic situation by prioritizing its own status. The country's position would perhaps not be so worthy of criticism if its influence were limited, or if its indicators were worrying.

But Germany's economy is one devoid of over-indebtedness, with excess private savings and a strong current-account surplus. It would have been more reasonable for Germany to adopt a more expansive fiscal policy, but in no way comparable with that of other countries with much more worrying macroeconomic data, countries that are Germany's financial and commercial customers. These economic policies have resulted in a credit crunch and a decline in aggregate demand, and this has deepened the recession.

For the reasons I have discussed, it is very difficult to change economic policy in such circumstances, given the utter ideological domination of neo-liberalism and its advocates. For Antón Costas and Xosé Carlos Arias,[35] four factors contribute to this. First, there are the interests of the finance industry and the inertia of old ideas. Second, the crisis has not yet renewed interest in collective involvement in public affairs, so factors affecting individuals come before those affecting the public at large.[36] Third, mistrust among more conservative quarters towards politics and the democratic state has pulled everything towards technocracy, towards an explosion of "professionals", such as in Italy and Greece, where executives, who despite their defects were democratically elected, have been replaced by unelected teams of technocrats from the circles of Goldman Sachs. And finally, there have been no political innovations – no progressive taxation measures – to help spread the wealth. The crossroads of the world economy is well lit, but politics is unable to negotiate it.

Notes

1. See J. de Vries, "The Limits of Globalization in the Early Modern World", *The Economic History Review*, 63/3 (2009): 710–33; J. Williamson, J. Rosés and K. O'Rourke, "Globalization, Growth and Distribution in Spain, 1500–1913", NBER working paper no. 13055, 2008; J. Williamson, M. Bordo and A.M. Taylor (eds.), *Globalization in Historical Perspective* (Chicago: Chicago University Press, 2006); J. Williamson and S. Pamuk, *The Mediterranean Response to Globalization before 1950* (London: Routledge, 2000). J. Williamson and K. O'Rourke, *Globalization and History: The Evolution of a Nineteenth-Century Atlantic Economy* (Cambridge: Cambridge University Press, 1999). See also a co-integration analysis that gives a detailed description of a common market for trading cereal crops

between the 16th and 18th centuries based on fluctuations in the prices of basic food items in the Spanish Mediterranean region in C. Manera and A. Sansó, "The Mediterranean Sea: A Bridge between Coasts: 18th Century Trading Links between the East Coast of Spain ant the Balearic Islands", in S. Cavaciocchi (ed.), *Ricchezza del mare, ricchezza dal mare, secc. XIII–XVIII* (Florence: Le Monnier, 2006), 179–99.; and in C. Manera, G. Jover, and A. Sansó, "Dock Cities and Cointegration Degree of Food markets in Europe, 1700–1811", working paper, *Third European Congress on World and Global History* (London: London School of Economics, 2011). Victoria N. Bateman also examines the trade of crops in this period, but looking at a wider picture in V. Bateman, "The Evolution of Markets in Early Modern Europe, 1350–1800: A Study of Grain Prices", *The Economic History Review*, 64/2 (2011): 447–71.

2. See: C. Rowley and J. Benson (eds.), *Globalization and Labour in the Asia Pacific Region* (London: Frank Cass, 2000); and C. Rowley, R. Fitzgerald and P. Stewart, *Managed in Hong Kong: Adaptive Systems, Entrepreneurship and Human Resources* (London: Frank Cass, 2000).

3. N. Lardy, *Integrating China into the Global Economy* (Washington DC: Brookings Institution Press, 2002); F. Lemoine, *L'économie de la Chine* (Paris: La Découverte, 2003); M. Renard, *China and its Regions: Economic Growth and Reform in Chinese Provinces* (Cheltenham: Edward Elgar, 2002). J. Studwell, *The China Dream: The Elusive Quest for the Greatest Untapped Market on Earth* (London: Profile Books, 2002).

4. The combination of deregulation of the economy, cuts to social services and large tax cuts for the rich are part of supply-side economics, a school so dear to neoconservatives. However, even David Stockman, who was Reagan's budget director and a firm believer in this school, was willing to admit in February 2011 that there was no evidence proving that tax cuts guaranteed growth, and he even added that growth was achieved once the tax burden was increased after 1982. The subsequent ultra-conservative fiscal policies of the two Bushes massively increased government debt to hard-to-sustain levels, which could reach 180% of GDP by 2035 (see J. Fontana, *Por el bien del imperio: una historia del mundo desde 1945* (Barcelona: Pasado y Presente, 2011), pp. 615–17.

5. Regarding Brenner see his classic "Agrarian Class Structure and Economic Development in Pre-Industrial Europe", *Past and Present*, 70 (1976): 30–75. and *Merchants and Revolution: Commercial Change, Political Conflict, and London's Overseas Traders, 1550–1653* (Princeton, NJ: Princeton University Press, 1993). Regarding the crisis see R. Brenner, *The Economics of Global Turbulence: The Advanced Capitalist*

Economies from Long Boom to Long Downturn, 1945–2005 (New York: Verso, 2006).

6. The periods determined in the Kondratieff waves are widely known, although also widely disputed. Each cycle is divided into an ascendant and a downward phase, so the movements within each phase are much shorter (Kitchin and Juglar). Amin, Gunder Frank and Jaffe emphasized the magnitude of technological change in the ascendant phase of the long-term cycle (50 to 60 years), a time when they believe the capitalist system was in a sense competing for its own survival. See S. Amin, A. Gunder Frank and H. Jaffe, *¿Cómo será 1984?: debate sobre la crisis y las tendencias actuales del capitalismo mundial* (Madrid: Zero, 1976).

7. The notion of systemic crisis – that is, a large, structurally deep crisis that raises questions regarding much of the economic system – is also defended by Guillermo de la Dehesa in *La primera gran crisis financiera del siglo XXI* (Madrid: Alianza, 2010), a work containing a wealth of facts and analyses that in its diagnosis calls for more efficient regulation and supervision. Amartya Sen, on the other hand, says we are not witnessing a systemic crisis, nor do we need to "re-engineer capitalism" – as the French president Nicolas Sarkozy once put it in a clear moment of panic. The eminent Indian economist believes we need to recover the ideas of the great Scottish economist Adam Smith related to the morality of human activity (the reference work is *The Theory of Moral Sentiments*, published in 1759, in which Smith proposes actions that go beyond mere financial gain). See A. Sen, "Capitalismo más allá de la crisis", *El Viejo Topo*, 255 (2009): 16–23.

8. R. Brenner, *The Boom and the Bubble: The US in the World Economy* (New York: Verso, 2002); J. O'Connor, *Accumulation Crisis* (Oxford: Basil Blackwell, 1984); E. Todd, *After the Empire: The Breakdown of the American Order* (New York: Columbia University Press, 2003); I.M. Wallerstein, G. Arrighi, and T.K. Hopkins, *Antisystemic Movements* (London: Verso, 1989).

9. I am following Brenner's arguments here.

10. "Great Recession" is the name that has stuck for the crisis that began in 2007–8. Carmen Reinhart and Kenneth Rogoff have also called it a "Great Contraction", in an analogy with the term "Great Depression" coined by Milton Friedman and Anna Schwartz for the 1930s crisis. Reinhart and Rogoff believe the word "contraction" better summarizes the complete collapse in the credit markets and asset prices and the fall in employment and production. See C.M. Reinhart and K.S. Rogoff, *This Time Is Different: Eight Centuries of Financial Folly* (Princeton, NJ: Princeton University Press, 2009). See also M. Friedman and A. Schwartz, *A Monetary History of the United States, 1867–1960*

(Princeton, NJ: Princeton University Press, 1963). General overviews can be found in G. Caballero and M.D. Garza (eds.), *La Gran Recesión: Perspectivas globales y regionales* (Coruña: Netbiblo, 2010); and A. Costas (coord.), *La crisis de 2008: De la economía a la política y más allá*, Mediterráneo Económico, 18 (2010).

11. See G.A. Akerlof, "The Market for 'Lemons': Quality Uncertainty and the Market Mechanism", *Quarterly Journal of Economics*, 84/ 3 (August 1970), 488–500; J. Stiglitz and A. Weiss, "Credit Rationing in Markets with Imperfect Information", *American Economic Review*, 71/3 (1981): 393–410.

12. Krugman's stance on this issue is in line with the theses defended by William Baumol in his renowned concept that economics literature has dubbed "Baumol's cost disease". Basically, Baumol argues that imbalances between sectors of the economy can lead to a relocation of resources, which are redirected towards activities with little or no growth, such as services, which stalls aggregate growth. For Baumol, the work factor explains the differences in productivity between sectors. He says that in what he calls the "progressive" sectors (those related to industry and manufacturing), work is an instrument, while in the "non-progressive" sectors (the services), it is usually an end in itself. In an economy where wages are set according to productivity growth, costs in non-progressive sectors will be higher than in industry. The "disease", therefore, is a downward trend in economic growth and aggregate productivity coupled with rising prices of services. W.J. Baumol, "Productivity Policy in the Service Sector", in R. Inman (ed.), *Managing the Service Economy: Prospects and Problems* (Cambridge: Cambridge University Press, 1985); and a broader analysis in A. Maroto and J.R. Cuadrado, *Los cambios estructurales y el papel del sector Servicios en la productividad española*, Servilab, Universidad de Alcalá, document 8/2006; and in English, A. Maroto and J.R. Cuadrado, "Is Services Growth an Obstacle to Productivity Growth? A Comparative Analysis", *Structural Change & Economic Dynamics*, 20/4 (2009): 254–65.

13. J. Stiglitz, *Globalization and its Discontents* (New York: W.W. Norton, 2002); J. Stiglitz, *The Roaring Nineties: A New History of the World's Most Prosperous Decade* (New York: W.W. Norton, 2003); J. Madrick, "Computers: Waiting for the Revolution", *New York Review of Books*, 45/4 (1998): 29–33; M. Castells, *The Rise of the Network Society*, 2nd edn., The Information Age: Economy, Society and Culture, i (Cambridge, MA: Blackwell, 2000); *The Power of Identity*, 2nd edn., The Information Age: Economy, Society and Culture, ii (Cambridge, MA: Blackwell, 2004); *End of Millenium*, 2nd edn., The Information Age: Economy, Society and Culture, iii (Cambridge, MA: Blackwell, 2000);

P. Krugman, *The Great Unraveling: Losing Our Way in the New Century* (New York: W.W. Norton, 2003).

14. C.P. Kindleberger, *Keynesianism versus Monetarism and Other Essays in Financial History* (London: HarperCollins, 1985); C.P. Kindleberger, *The World in Depression, 1929–1939*, rev. and enlarged edn. (Berkeley, CA: University of California Press, 1986).

15. See K.J Arrow and G. Debreu, "The Existence of an Equilibrium for a Competitive Economy", *Econometrica*, 22 (1954): 265–90.

16. J. Stiglitz and A. Weiss, "Credit Rationing in Markets with Imperfect Information", *American Economic Review*, 71/3 (1981): 393–410.

17. See R.C.K. Burdekin and P.L. Siklos, *Deflation: Current and Historical Perspectives* (Cambridge: Cambridge University Press, 2004). The authors of this work argue that a fall in consumption can greatly affect prices in both developed and emerging countries, and that this scenario is much more worrying than inflationary pressures.

18. It has often been repeated that the economist Nouriel Roubini, in a speech he delivered at the World Economic Forum in Davos in 2006, was the first to warn that a major economic crisis was imminent and would have drastic consequences for Europe's peripheral countries: http://www.stern.nyu.edu/nroubini. See also N. Roubini and S. Mihm, *Crisis Economics: A Crash Course in the Future of Finance* (New York: Penguin Press, 2010). However, in Spain the economist and environmental expert José Manuel Naredo had already written papers long before the crisis warning of the difficulties of maintaining an economic structure held up by a bloated construction sector and the resulting speculation on the property market. As an introduction, see J.M. Naredo, *La burbuja inmobiliario-financiera en la coyuntura económica reciente (1985–1995)* (Madrid: Siglo XXI, 1998); and J.M. Naredo, "Claves de la globalización financiera y de la presente crisis internacional", *Estudis d'Història Econòmica*, 19 (2002): 201–15.

19. A bibliographical perspective on the financial crisis, which serves as a guide for this section, is provided in A. Carbajo, "Ortodoxias y heterodoxias sobre la crisis financiera", *Revista de Libros*, 169 (2011): 3–7.

20. See M. Lewis, *The Big Short: Inside the Doomsday Machine* (New York: W.W. Norton, 2010). From a more journalistic perspective, see A.R. Sorkin, *Too Big to Fail: The Inside Story of How Wall Street and Washington Fought to Save the Financial System* (New York: Viking, 2009), in which the author emphasizes that decisions made by major economic leaders (such as the US Treasury Secretary) are totally improvised and are taken based on the avalanche of events happening minute by minute. And you get the impression they don't have a clue what's happening. The

most striking thing about these practices is that they affect the very top of the economic hierarchy.

21. G. Stern and R.J. Feldman, *Too Big to Fail: The Hazards of Bank Bailouts* (Washington: Brookings Institution Press, 2004).

22. C.M. Reinhart and K.S. Rogoff, *This Time Is Different: Eight Centuries of Financial Folly* (Princeton, NJ: Princeton University Press, 2009).

23. Excess savings are also related to growing income inequalities caused by the neo-liberal era, as can be inferred from the 2011 OECD report *Economic Outlook*, 90 (2011).

24. One fascinating author, Max Otte, in his very blunt but precise style, argues that the eurozone needs somehow to be segmented. He says Greece, Ireland, Portugal and Spain should be separated, with their debt partially cancelled, and then their national currencies should be reintroduced so they can adopt their own economic policy with an unequivocal focus on currency devaluation strategies to make their economies more competitive. See M. Otte, *Stoppt das Euro-Desaster* (Berlin: Ullstein Buchverlage, 2010); M. Otte, *Die Krise halt sich nicht an Regeln: 99 Fragen zur aktuellen Situation – und wie es weitergeht* (Berlin: Econ, 2010).

25. J. Stiglitz, *Freefall: America, Free Markets, and the Sinking of the World Economy* (New York: W.W. Norton, 2010). Excellent explanations of the whole picture can be found in J. Fontana, *Por el bien del imperio: una historia del mundo desde 1945*, pp. 931 et seq.; and F. Comín, *Historia económica mundial* (Madrid: Alianza Editorial, 2011), pp. 709 et seq.

26. There were two essential causes of the Japanese economic bubble: deregulation of the banks and monetary policy. These are the very same causes of the current crisis in the main Western economies. See S. Tsuzu, *Japan's Capitalism: Creative Defeat and Beyond*, Canto edn. (Cambridge: Cambridge University Press, 1996); A. Horiuchi: "A Bank Crisis in a Bank-Centered Financial System: The Japanese Experience since the 1990s", working paper, Chuo University; A. Torrero, "El final de la burbuja especulativa y la crisis econòmica de Japón", in *Observatorio de la Economía y la Sociedad del Japón*, 3 (2011).

27. In this respect, Gaspar Feliu and Carles Sudrià stressed that the 1931 and 1932 banking crises were recurrent. The administration's passivity was due to a belief that it was appropriate to clean up the financial sector. Everyone therefore thought that letting banks that had engaged in speculation collapse would be a good thing. The problem with this strategy, as Feliu and Sudrià point out, is that it means the innocent pay for the sins of the guilty. A second factor to consider is the gold standard that was in place at the time. If the Federal Reserve wanted to maintain convertibility between US dollars and gold, it was

extremely limited in the amount of credit it could grant. The very crisis fuelled demand for conversions and forced restrictive policies to be maintained. Britain's abandonment of the gold standard in 1931 put tremendous pressure on the dollar, which led to an even tougher monetary policy. In that situation, only policies to stimulate demand, i.e. directly related to the real, productive economy, would provide a way out of the crisis. However, a change of presidency, among other measures, was needed first. See G. Feliu and C. Sudrià, *Introducció a la història econòmica mundial* (Universitat de València–Universitat de Barcelona, 2006), especially pp. 343 et seq.

28. Data taken from Deutsche Bundesbank and from La Caixa's, *Monthly Report*, 331 (2010).

29. The financial crises have fuelled a series of publications that attempt to reveal the mechanisms that spread viral attacks from one economy to another. A recent assessment, with a lengthy econometric analysis, can be found in M. Dungey, R.A. et al., *Transmission of Financial Crises and Contagion* (Oxford: Oxford University Press, 2011); R.W. Kolb (ed.), *Financial Contagion. The Viral Threat to the Wealth of Nations* (Hoboken, NJ: John Wiley & Sons, 2011).

30. H. Minsky, *Stabilizing an Unstable Economy* (New York: McGraw-Hill, 2008); H. Minsky, *John Maynard Keynes* (New York: McGraw-Hill, 2008).

31. Countries like Spain and Canada, which have stricter regulations preventing banks from taking on toxic assets like the American junk mortgages, were better at resisting the contamination produced by the globalization of the financial crisis. But things took a turn for the worse in Spain, because its banks were dependent on the performance of the property markets, which were expanding strongly everywhere. See J. García Montalvo, *De la quimera inmobiliaria al colapso financiero* (Barcelona: Antoni Bosch Editor, 2009).

32. G.A. Akerlof and R.J. Shiller, *Animal Spirits* (Princeton, NJ: Princeton University Press, 2009). This book gives a damning analysis of failed economic theories based on an over-optimistic view of how the markets work. The authors base the revival of the Keynesian idea of "animal spirits" on five essential pillars: confidence, fairness, corruption, money illusions and stories deriving from economic processes. Thus, the authors claim the psychological, human perspective explains many of the irrational behaviours found in economics.

33. See R. Skidelsky, "The Boom was the Illusion", *New Statesman*, 5074, 20, at
<http://www.newstatesman.com/economy/2011/10/world-growth-china -investment>, accessed 20 July 2012. Regarding Hayek see

B. Caldwell, "Hayek, Friedrich August von (1899–1992)" in S.N. Durlauf and L.E. Blume (eds.), *The New Palgrave Dictionary of Economics*, 2nd edn. (Basingstoke: Palgrave Macmillan, 2008); regarding Keynes, an essential read is R. Skidelsky, *The Return of the Master* (London: Allen Lane, 2009).

34. R. Skidelsky, *The Return of the Master*. As you would expect, Skidelsky proposes a much more profound theory on the present-day relevance of the great Cambridge economist's ideas. Skidelsky goes beyond the occasional, often shoddy, references to Keynes and his works. One need only look at the two major contributions Keynes made to the Bretton Woods Agreements: despite losing the negotiations, he was influential through his contributions on exchange-rate adjustments (i.e. moving away from the inherent rigidity of the gold standard), which enabled currency devaluations, and on control of capital movements. Keynes's deep reflection on the 1930s crisis enabled him to make these two contributions, which were vital to the post-war global economic recovery.

35. A. Costas and X.C. Arias, *La torre de la arrogancia: Políticas y mercados después de la tormenta* (Barcelona: Ariel, 2011).

36. This idea of excessive individualism in today's societies is also prominent in the writings of the influential philosopher Zygmunt Bauman, who introduced the interesting concept of "liquid modernity". Regarding the topic at hand, Bauman explains that the super-individuality of this "liquid modernity" generates fears and reduces one's capacity to deal with adversity. He says the *indignados* protest movement in Spain is fuelled by emotion but lacks thought. "Without thought", he says, "you get nowhere." This notion is valid for predicting the future (a job normally required of economists), but Bauman's conclusions are not very encouraging: he says nothing can be predicted, everything changes, and what really matters is the present. See Z. Bauman, *44 Letters from the Liquid Modern World* (Cambridge: Polity, 2010); and Z. Bauman, *Collateral Damage: Social Inequalities in a Global Age* (Cambridge: Polity, 2011), in which the author presents a more collective vision and warns of the danger of social exclusion and a loss of cohesion among those he labels the "marginal class". He says they are the collateral damage of the crisis, since they are completely separated from the policy of wealth redistribution. This marginal class suffers from the cuts to public services, welfare and extremely lax taxation, which reduces government income.

Chapter 3

Orthodoxy versus Heterodoxy
Inflation, Unemployment, Growth, Profit

1. Does the focus on prices mean ignoring unemployment?

The evolution of the economic crisis is placing the discipline in a cloudy, turbulent place. Economists' predictions regarding economic and financial decisions that will be taken to relieve the crisis are not even close to being accurate. The tools available are not sufficient and have proved to be totally powerless in the times in which we are now living. Government ministers around the world, research centres, prestigious university departments, and prestigious members of the intellectual and political elite are still shooting in the dark in ever-changing circumstances that are difficult to predict. The perceptions – little more than perceptions – that filter through to consumers are that the measures taken will bring the desired results, and light will appear at the end of the tunnel. Economists' arrogance could not be more pronounced: they try to convincingly and coherently explain that the multi-phase roadmap is in place and will lead us to the end of the problem once those phases are behind us. This belief prevents any possible understanding or influence from other social or experimental sciences. The petulance leads people to believe that with all the mathematical tools it has available, economics alone can solve doubts and uncertainties. That is a great fallacy.

Economic theory is in a certain state of "normality", in the sense of its ability to predict the behaviours of people and economic players, who act based on the principles of utilitarianism, the notions of equilibrium points and the rationality of actions. However, those processes are often difficult to explain and therefore difficult to map as clear sequences of events, but could perhaps be understood if other parameters were involved. Economics has always maintained strong links with technological changes. It should be noted that this perspective, in which technology becomes the famous Prometheus unleashed, should be accompanied by everything that affects institutional frameworks – factors that are not always tangible, but that do spur growth. However, the major routes are found in the knowledge of past developments: the analytical capacity that determines the past to identify long-term patterns that help us understand processes occurring today.

In this context, the economic crisis has already inspired numerous and varied contributions to the literature.[1] This crisis, this reality, changes over time, and the diagnoses made in different spheres have no option but to change too. In the more serious contributions, two major positions emerge. Some authors say the current crisis is unusual, unprecedented, and different from all the major economic crises of the past. Others argue that there are regularities in the way crises evolve, so in the current crisis we know how the waves of technological change will be assimilated. Some viewpoints even distil doses of optimism in the face of the current cataclysm. In her magnificent book on financial capital and technological changes,[2] Carlota Pérez concludes that the current crisis is marking a transition from a wild, turbulent golden age run by financial capital to a more harmonious period driven by production capital in an institutional framework that is more inclined towards the real economy. This is certainly an innovative idea, a welcome change from the downpour of defeatist messages and bad news if the guidelines set by the IMF, the ECB and the European Commission are not adhered to (guidelines which, right now, provide few signs that the economy will recover and be discharged from the intensive care unit).

The sense of constant improvisation caused by a lack of economic planning and an inability to plan ahead for more than even a few weeks created uncertainty in society. There are some voices crying in the wilderness – economists and social scientists of an academic mould – warning of the folly of Europe's economic policy.[3] It is a policy that responds specifically to the interests of the German and French economies, but has one very worrying feature: the lack of a true leadership in a Europe that ought to increasingly be seen as a major world region rather than as a fragmented group of states with different interests. Basically there are two major positions regarding economic schools of thought applied to the real economy: the neo-Keynesian viewpoints, exemplified in the works of Krugman and in more resolute works such as those of Stiglitz, which emphasize economic growth to reduce unemployment, even though it can lead to inflationary pressures; and the viewpoint that has prevailed, led by the ECB, in which the main concern is to contain inflation and reduce budget deficits, the ultimate goal being balanced budgets. It is important to note that concern for budget deficits is not unique to more orthodox positions: everyone knows perennial or very severe deficits are unsustainable. But those of us with – let's say – a more heterodox perspective also know that balanced budgets should not be sought after religiously, regardless of the cost, as suggested in the more conservative discourse on both sides of the Atlantic.

Institutions like the IMF, the ECB and many finance ministries and private banks in the world's richest countries are sending out unequivocal calls for strict control of prices to be addressed urgently, given its intrinsic relationship with how the budget deficit and government debt evolves. These messages allow very little room for nuances or interpretations, stating categorically that price stability is the essential factor that guarantees economic growth and therefore plays a key role in enabling countries to achieve good living standards. Nevertheless, inflation, which nobody doubts needs to be kept under control, requires a much deeper analysis to avoid over-mechanical, over-simplistic applications for the present situation. We mustn't, as Paul Samuelson put it, base economic policy on "shibboleths" – that is, hard and fast slogans that take over serious, thoughtful discussion and exchange of opinions. Especially since in economics slogans become hallmarks that are constantly repeated, and this repetition gets in the way of the obvious truth.[4] This trend has led to the sale of intellectual products with no scientific backing. A case in point is David H. Fischer's book on prices.[5] Addressing business leaders, he asserts categorically that economic cycles and crises have ended, but the actual economic events have disproved this. As Robert Solow warns, there is not one set of laws of economics applicable to all times and all places, and the part of economics that is not dependent upon economic history and the social context is very small and of little interest.[6]

Indeed, as we have already discussed, EU recommendations lean towards strict control of inflation, with the commendable objective of keeping the economy competitive. In Spain, currency devaluation – so effective in the past at times when the economy was less competitive due to disparities in inflation rates – is no longer used. Today's scenario is quite different, and prices, and therefore inflation, have become the key indicator that should cause most concern, since if year-on-year inflation is projected to rise it generates all kinds of anxieties and uncertainties. However, cases studied from economic history, especially in the United States, show that moderate inflation is not necessarily negative. Quite the opposite: it can even benefit economic structures. In other words, controlled inflation that is kept below 4% is a good compromise if growth is positive and unemployment in decline. Some of the most prestigious American academic economists have examined this idea, which is somewhat of a break from the more widely accepted, more orthodox interpretations of economic developments.

The 2001 Nobel Prize in Economics winner George Akerlof wrote in 1996, in an article about the American economy co-authored with William Dickens and George Henry, that the cost of keeping inflation low, as close as possible to zero, would result in negative growth, and recommended that completely stable prices should in no circumstances be the Federal Reserve's main objective. Akerlof wasn't criticizing price control. In fact, he unashamedly praised it. But he was questioning the obsession for achieving a rate of inflation close to zero, especially when unemployment was rather high, at around 6% when his article was published. His theory is that reducing inflation when it is high increases unemployment very little, so it is better to keep inflation low, which improves forecasts since it barely raises the number of unemployed. However, when there is a certain level of productivity and you try to keep inflation low – bearing in mind the German hyperinflation in the 1920s, which is still an awful memory – the costs in terms of employment are very high. The main reason, according to Akerlof, is that inflation that is too low has high political and social costs, since companies are against wage cuts in certain circumstances. In fact, it seems employers rarely cut wages since they fear it could knock the company's and its leaders' morale. In other words, bringing inflation down to 3% is cheap in terms of employment, but if inflation dips below 3% the costs shoot up. The authors draw on economic history, and specifically the 1929 crisis and its repercussions, to give a more convincing argument for their model, and they stress that in terms of prices and employment, the strong negative inflation was accompanied by massive unemployment, affecting a quarter of America's workforce.[7] Peter Temin's research confirms this, showing that the stubborn policy of wanting to maintain the gold standard was one of the main factors that made the Great Depression last so long. The monetary and fiscal authorities introduced contractionary policies, whereas today's 20/20 hindsight shows that expansionary policies were needed. However, any alternative approach had to fit into the gold standard system, which politicians and economists claimed was untouchable but which was shaken by the harsh reality. The alternatives to the gold standard were not taken seriously, neither by government when they were put forward, nor by investors or consumers when they were introduced. Everyone believed they were folly compared to the stability offered by the monetary standard.[8]

Paul Krugman made similar arguments to Akerlof's, breaking away from the prevalent viewpoint of academia.[9] The 2008 Nobel Prize winner argues that the benefits of price stability are relative. Once again, Krugman bases his arguments on the lessons learned from economic history: the major American recession in the 1980s, which pushed down prices by 4–10%, occurred after a long period of high unemployment and excess capacity. The data are very clear: in the United States, the 1979 unemployment rate was not achieved again until 1988 (it was higher for almost a decade), so there was a sacrifice, a huge cost of almost a trillion dollars to achieve a very small long-term gain. The author's conclusions are startling: the belief that completely stable prices are a blessing that provides major benefits at very little cost rests more on faith than on evidence. The real effects of stable prices, with inflation close to zero, are tiny gains that are more than cancelled out by side effects that punish the economy. Krugman analyses simple correlations to support his assumptions: first between economic growth and job creation between 1980 and 1995, with results showing that growth cut unemployment; and second between inflation and unemployment from 1985 to 1995, finding that there is no correlation at all. So, the slogan the leading author coined is simple but eloquent: growth cut unemployment, inflation didn't. On this point, Akerlof and Krugman owe much to Arthur Okun:[10] the relationship between growth and job creation is one of the few "laws", if indeed there are any laws, that exist in economic science, and it was Okun who developed this law. Reducing inflation had a significant negative effect on wages, incomes and living standards between 1979 and 1990, as shown by Samuel Bowles, David M. Gordon and Thomas E. Weisskopf, using monetary indicators and other indicators related to what we call "human development".[11]

Stiglitz takes a similar standpoint. A country can have low inflation but zero growth and high unemployment. According to Stiglitz – who also won the 2001 Nobel Prize in Economics alongside Akerlof – most economists agree that such a country would be in a disastrous macroeconomic position. They believe inflation is more a means than an end: since inflation that is too high often results in poor growth, which in turn leads to high unemployment, inflation is systematically stigmatized. In his critique, Stiglitz refers to the positions held by the IMF with respect to poor countries and the remedies it invariably and acritically applies to those countries' economic structures, under the distant supervision of its bureaucrats.[12] However, since Stiglitz published his contributions, the IMF has adopted different approaches. One of its reports in February 2010 warned critically against over-confidence in monetary policy rather than fiscal policy and called for a more flexible rate of inflation (which should be increased from 2% to 4%) to give macroeconomic policies more leeway.[13]

It is true that there are serious contributors to economics literature whose arguments are very different from those I have discussed so far. Indeed, it is their discourse that is prominent in economics when the relationships between prices, inflation and growth are discussed. And it is essentially this viewpoint that is taught in most university economics departments. But I believe it is interesting to discuss these other viewpoints, which could serve as an incentive to analyse other cases in greater detail, provided that they are built on equally well-founded and well-respected discourses in applied economics and can effectively and tangibly be translated into policy. In this regard, one should remember that in 1996, the US presidency adopted the conclusions advocated by Akerlof, Dickens and Perry for the theory on the decline in inflation, which, as I have shown, had a positive effect on Clinton's economic policy during his final years of office.

2. The need for growth

There is thus a kind of conflict among major economic variables, which are interpreted in many different ways. Naturally, however, no economist or economic policymaker is willing to renounce economic growth or degrowth.[14] The difficulty lies in deciding which levers need activating most to trigger a recovery. One of the positions adopted is the major ideology that is most prominent among the neo-liberal school of thought. Because when people talk about orthodoxy, that is precisely what they mean: a balanced budget come what may, strict control of the budget deficit, constant praise for legal certainty as a kind of all-powerful mantra, a smaller public sector (requiring cuts to public services, and the recurring idea of economic freedom. The cornerstone of this economic viewpoint is that the market is always efficient, and many kinds of contributions have been published to try to justify this position, which still holds that points of equilibrium eventually form when there is an open economy. The same authors also insist that government intervention is usually harmful and undesirable.

In times of economic crisis, the dichotomy between keeping accounts "in good health" (i.e. balanced, adjusted according to income) and fostering stimulus strategies (even if it means working under the umbrella of deficit and debt) has formed a set of crossroads for politicians and the economists who advise them. At such times it is also common to hear that the crisis is something unknown, with aspects not seen before, which to a large extent determines the responses made. The highly improvised nature of these responses is nearly always criticized, but is perfectly understandable. Anyone who believes that the person in charge of a country's or a company's finance or economy always has the perfect way out of all possible scenarios is mistaken. Those who claim they do are lying. The crisis leads to spasmodic movements on the stock and financial markets, which pervade production. This in turn leads to vague, spontaneous, often immature replies. Such misguided behaviour is caused by the lack of knowledge of economic history, since the unique features of each economic crisis still follow certain regular patterns that can be spotted from a historical perspective. The current Chairman of the Federal Reserve, Ben Bernanke, is a leading expert on the 1929 crisis and has published works of great scientific value on the topic.[15] His wisdom helped him make certain decisions around September 2008 with the fall of Lehman Brothers. One important decision was to inject liquidity into the system to avoid short-circuiting the flow of credit. The Federal Reserve was resolute, and thus prevented even greater shocks to the American financial system, and therefore to much of the world. Another question altogether is what the financial system should give in return for being held together by taxpayers. This is another reform that should be debated and tackled without delay.

Whatever the criticisms that can be levelled at the present behaviour of the Federal Reserve, the policy adopted by Bernanke was followed by none of his predecessors during the 1929 crisis. None except one vital figure. There is one little-known period in the economic history of the Wall Street crash in which the prominent figure was a small, Utah Mormon banker by the name of Marriner S. Eccles. It is not unusual for people who were key figures in the past, who were innovative in the decisions they took and visionary in one form or another, to be rediscovered at a later time having passed almost unnoticed in between, with contemporaries of theirs having claimed all the fame.[16] I have no intention of reviewing the causes of the 1929 crisis and how it panned out, but I would like to draw attention to the economic debates that took place, which were very similar to those taking place today: the dilemma was whether to adopt an orthodox policy or explore other ways of dealing with the depression.[17] It was in this context of uncertainty that Eccles emerged, a "small, slender man with dark eyes and a pale, sharp face" as Robert B. Reich described him, and a man who was Keynesian before Keynes himself.[18]

Eccles ran a small banking institution, but his career path led him to amass a large fortune. The Wall Street crash in October 1929 took many economic sectors by surprise; much the same happened in

2008, when international bodies and all the world's governments were predicting sustained economic growth and were ignoring the clear signs of a slowdown until the whole thing erupted in September 2008 when, as we have already seen, major US banks went bankrupt. The fall of the banks was an eye-opener. In the 1930s, discussions focused on whether to protect the financial system or let it collapse. Many of the philosophical elements of liberal economics were at stake, including the gold standard, which had helped keep the international markets balanced. Both Peter Temin and Charles P. Windleberger have written enlightening chapters on the whole affair, and Carmen M. Reinhart, Kenneth S. Rogoff and Carlos Marichal have made interesting contributions from the field of social science, adding the depth of economic history as a crucial piece to understanding what is happening right now.[19] The conclusion is most striking: everything we're seeing in the media, in specialist articles, in debates among professionals and in politicians' speeches has all been seen before. There's nothing new at all.[20]

But let us turn back to the Mormon banker Eccles. In the heat of the controversy regarding how best to tackle the crisis, Eccles, who had concrete experience in the banking market, understood that refusing loans and shutting off the credit tap would make the depression even deeper. Furthermore, the businessman, who because of his family background and ideology had always believed the state should not interfere with the economy, stated in 1933 that the only plausible way out of the crisis was to allocate more money to unemployment benefits, public works, farms and refinancing mortgages. He believed this would require taking monetary powers away from regional financial bodies and centralizing them within the Federal Reserve Board of Governors, and giving government the capacity to boost public spending. According to Eccles, liquidity was the only measure of the usefulness of money, so you had to give money a social purpose while helping it to circulate through investments and transactions. And it is the federal government – with the power to issue money or request capital – that can channel efforts to generate the demand urgently needed for a recovery. In other words, with the heavy recession, the budget deficit was becoming the only appropriate formula to inject this capital into the system and improve the stagnant economy.[21] All these recommendations were made three

Table 3.1 Deficit and debt of some European countries as percentages of GDP

Country	Deficit to GDP			Debt to GDP		
	2009	2010	2011	2009	2010	2011
Germany	−3.4	−5	−4.6	73.1	76.7	79.7
Austria	−4.3	−5.5	−5.3	69.1	73.9	77
Belgium	−5.9	−5.8	−5.8	97.2	101.2	104
Spain	11.2	−10.1	−9.3	54.3	66.3	74
France	−8.3	−8.2	−7.7	76.1	82.5	87.6
Greece	−12.7	−12.2	−12.8	112.6	124.9	135.4
Netherlands	−4.7	−6.1	−5.6	59.8	65.6	69.7
Ireland	12.5	−14.7	−14.7	65.8	82.9	96.2
Italy	−5.3	−5.3	−5.1	114.6	116.7	117.8
Portugal	8	−8	−8.7	77.4	84.6	91.1
Eurozone	−6.4	−6.9	−6.5	78.2	84	88.2
EU–27	−6.9	−7.5	−6.9	73	79.3	83.7

Source: By the author based on European Commission data.

years before John Keynes published his *General Theory*. There is a very clear, twofold lesson to learn from this: sticking doggedly to a certain type of economic policy has not always given satisfactory results, while considering new measures has led to tangible improvements.

Spain is a case in point. Measures to boost the Spanish economy had been in place for quite a while, and were backed up by relatively healthy public finances, as shown in Table 3.1, especially for 2009.

Spain was enjoying a significant budget surplus compared to the negative average for the eurozone (−6.4%) and the 27-member EU (−6.9%). Also, its national debt was below the Maastricht Treaty limit, and more than twenty percentage points below the EU average. In other words, as the crisis was taking off in earnest and the lethal consequences had not yet set in, 2009 closed with the Spanish economy in a much more promising state than that of other, more powerful countries. A wave of measures had been introduced to reduce the impact of the credit crunch that were slowly but surely working (the "Plan E" for the construction sector through local councils, support for car sales, support for long-term unemployed people, the investment lines of the Spanish government's Official Credit Institute (ICO), etc.). The measures compensated the sluggish private

Figure 3.1 Spanish Economic Growth: European Commission forecasts, 2005–2013

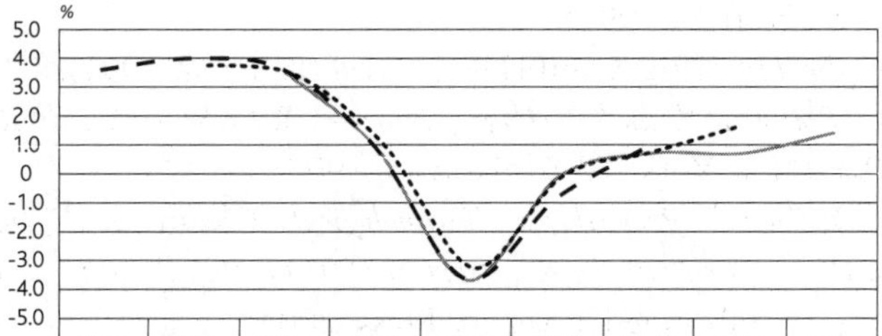

	2005	2006	2007	2008	2009	2010	2011	2012	2013	
– – Oct. 09	3.6	4.0	3.6	0.9	-3.7	-0.8	1.0			– – Oct. 09
····· Oct. 10		4.0	3.6	0.9	-3.7	-0.2	0.7	1.7		····· Oct. 10
—— Oct. 11			3.5	0.9	-3.7	-0.1	0.7	0.7	1.4	—— Oct. 11

Source: By the author based on European Commission data.

investment, which had a serious lack of circulating capital and, obviously, difficulties with obtaining preferential credits for investment policies.

Throughout this process, government spending as a percentage of GDP continued the upward trend that began in the 1970s. The starting point for the Spanish economy was not good: almost 20% in the five-year period from 1970 to 1974, nearly twenty points below the EU average, and thirteen below the OECD average. The government stepped up its spending considerably during Spain's political and economic transitions, as shown in Table 3.2 and the accompanying graph, before reducing it by six percentage points between 1995 and 2004. Spending began to increase again in 2005, reaching 47.2% in 2010 (although the 2010 figures are still provisional). This figure places Spain almost two percentage points below the EU-15 average, and just over two points above the OECD average. It is a level of spending similar to Germany's, but still far behind France's, Sweden's and the UK's. Therefore, the margins of spending cuts have different bases, so the sacrifices required of member states reveal different paths and therefore different capacities to cope with strict austerity measures. This is clear to see in Table 3.3, which lists indicators from 1970 to 2005. In 2005 (and probably in 2010 too), Spain

Table 3.2 Government spending, 1970–2010, as percentages of GDP (five-year averages)

Countries	1970–74	1975–79	1980–84	1985–89	1990–94	1995–99	2000–2004	2005–2009	2010
Germany	36.75	42.93	43.37	41.41	45.98	49.7	47.22	46.69	48.4
United States	32.33	33.28	35.74	36.67	37.88	35.61	35.78	36.53	41.5
Spain	19.95	23.89	33.23	39.56	43.84	41.13	38.68	39.29	47.2
France	32.67	39.98	45.22	46.42	49.26	53.58	52.62	54.29	55.4
Italy	36.22	40.71	47.46	50.98	54.23	30.24	47.34	47.16	51
Japan	24.82	30.41	34.39	32.55	33.52	38.56	38.27	35.56	41.1
UK	60.71	63.56	55.63	45.47	44.7	41.88	41.84	44.87	53.4
Sweden	48.44	58.55	67.91	64.41	67.31	62.89	57.2	56.42	56
EU-15	39.94	45.38	47.74	46.66	49.11	48.86	46.93	47.67	49
OECD-25	33.56	37.08	39.46	39.12	40.51	20.28	39.49	39.35	44.8

Source: E. Cereijo and F.J. Velázquez, *El stock de gasto público en los países de la OCDE* (Madrid: FUNCAS, 2008) and OECD.

Figure 3.2 Government spending, 1970–2010, as percentages of GDP (five-year averages) in Spain, EU-15 and OECD-25

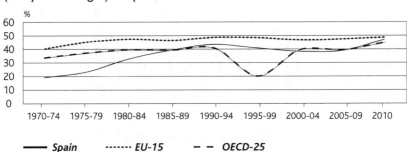

Source: E. Cereijo and F.J. Velázquez, *El stock de gasto público en los países de la OCDE* (Madrid: FUNCAS, 2008) and OECD. *Note:* 2010 data are provisional.

was spending significantly less than the EU average on health, education and social security, and much less than the biggest European economies. Even if we look further afield and compare Spain with the OECD (which includes countries with very different political, social and economic situations such as Mexico and South Korea), Spanish spending on health and education is still below average and spending on social security is only slightly above average.

In early 2010, the general diagnoses issued by the non-governmental institutions with the most meticulous economic forecasts said that Spanish economic growth was performing better than predicted for the final quarter of 2009, even saying that the downturn was slowing. The improved performance, according to the institutions, was thanks to the slowdown in the fall of retail sales and improved consumer confidence. Meanwhile, there was an unexpected fall in industrial production, which in March 2009 had been expected to recover. Production capacity did begin to recover thanks to the upturn in spending by foreign tourists coming to Spain from countries whose economy had already improved. Ten million euros were invested in the ICO to provide liquidity to companies working on sustainability projects. The current-account balance was reduced (to little over 6% by September 2009). Prices were kept down. And finally, there was a slowdown in the rate at which unemployment was growing, while there were signs of a boost to the jobs market.[22]

Table 3.3 Government spending by function, 1970–2005, as percentages of GDP (five-year averages)

Spending by function	Spain	Germany	France	Italy	UK	Sweden	EU-15	OECD-25
General public services	5.2	5.43	6.99	9.42	7.86	9.24	7.26	6.14
Defence	1.26	2.05	2.7	1.33	4.64	3.1	2.51	3.11
Public order and safety	1.15	1.5	1	1.89	2.2	1.05	1.51	1.53
Economic affairs	4.42	4.59	2.94	5.39	4.36	5.17	4.6	4.49
Environment protection	0.7	0.79	0.52	0.71	0.76	0.18	0.68	0.74
Housing and comm. amenities	0.82	0.86	1.3	1.06	1.84	2.1	1.18	0.98
Health	4.35	5.44	5.02	5.73	5.84	6.06	5.32	5.06
Recreation and culture	0.88	0.72	0.87	0.82	0.8	1.87	0.87	0.5
Education	3.31	4.14	5.84	4.94	5.9	8.57	5.18	5.25
Social protection	12.37	18.47	18.76	15.47	16.2	23.49	17.3	10.73
Total	34.46	43.99	45.92	46.75	50.38	60.83	46.41	38.52

Source: E. Cereijo and F.J. Velázquez, *El stock de gasto público en los países de la OCDE* (Madrid: FUNCAS, 2008) and OECD.

Figure 3.1 provides a summary of the process: despite all the difficulties in 2009, which is when the downward curve is steepest and
there was a latent danger of the dreaded L-shaped recession, the variables began to recover to form a tenuous but tangible V shape.
Nevertheless, the signs were very superficial, responding to a period
in which there was a big increase in public spending. This additional
public spending should have been accompanied by joint, coordinated
policies by the main European economic institutions to help the flow
of credit, thus boosting private investment. Table 3.3 reveals just
how fragile those data were, as Spain lost its entire surplus in a year
and turned it into a big deficit in 2010, exceeding the EU average.[23]
The failure of the Spanish growth model, built around a construction
sector that was infected by perverse speculative practices fuelled by
excessively lax lending policies (despite the greater regulation in the
Spanish financial system), resulted in redundancies and devastated
the economy when tax revenue plummeted and spending linked to
automatic stabilizers rose, thus widening the deficit and debt.

3. Profit indicator

It is widely known that under the capitalist system capital investment in new production methods arises when a certain amount of
profit is expected. If expansion continues but profits do not meet forecasts, the end result is obvious: investment stops, and as expansion
grinds to a halt, the negative chain reactions escalate. This reduces
demand for machinery, raw materials and labour, and eventually
sends unemployment sky high. This very synthetic process takes a
crucial factor into account that the dominant economic approach has
ignored in recent years: the existence of a cycle as an essential part of
the accumulation process, and the confirmation of uneven periodic
depressions resulting from the perennial need for investment, which
goes beyond the conditions that determine profits based on accumu-
lated capital.[24] In this respect, Karl Marx said that capitalism hadn't
reached the limits of its capacity to increase production forces, but
rather the uneven rate of growth instigated periodic crises that,
sooner or later, would show themselves to be incompatible with the
mode of production used to push the economy forward, resulting in

serious social conflicts.[25] In other words, capitalism becomes unproductive when the essential contradiction in the economic system is identified: the struggle between the development of production forces and the return on capital. This becomes manifest in a wide range of situations, so trying to find clearly defined patterns all too often results in frustration. It is by analysing economic history that one can better understand the crises that take place over time. On this crucial aspect, it is important to note the following points, in line with Marx's ideas mentioned above:

(A) Economic recessions drastically reduce profits. Indeed, there is a strong agreement on this among both Keynesian economists and Marxian economists like Maurice Dobb and Michal Kalecki. A fall in profits is seen as the inevitable cause of capitalist crises.[26] As I have already argued, this is directly related to economic cycles, so the idea of profits is associated not only with short-term, one-off phenomena, but also with more long-term events. The issue is of great interest regarding the different viewpoints on the nature of the Great Recession: here too there are lines of research that go beyond financial descriptions and delve deeper into the structural factors of the economic system. In this respect, the Kalecki model is suitable both for its simplicity and its content. John King describes it thus:[27]

$$B = C + A$$
$$C = C' + \lambda B$$
$$\text{hence } B = C' + A + \lambda B;$$
$$\text{therefore}$$
$$B = (C' + A)/(1 - \lambda)$$

"Real gross profit (B) . . . is the sum of capitalist consumption (C) and accumulation (A) [which is equivalent to gross capital formation, or in simple terms, investment]. Consumption by capitalists consists of a constant part (C1) and a variable part that is proportional to real gross profits (B). . . . [The equation] tells us that real gross profit is proportional to the aggregate expenditure of capitalists on consumption and accumulation. . . .

Since capitalist consumption is 'not very elastic', it follows that the principal factor causing fluctuations in aggregate profits is changes in investment activity. Kalecki maintained that investment decisions depend on the expected net yield."

According to Kalecki's formula, investment orders (*I*) are a positive function of capitalists' expenditure (C^1 + A) and a negative function of the existing capital stock (*K*):

$$I = m \, (C^1 + A) - nK$$

The relationship between the net profit and the change in the interest rate determines a company's propensity to invest and their strategies to obtain the necessary credit.

Clearly, then, the economy is unstable. Variabilities in investment have a substantial influence, a multiplying effect, in determining how total production will evolve. In a clever play on words, Kalecki said "investment is not only produced but also producing". King added, "Investment expenditure increases aggregate demand, which improves business conditions and stimulates further increases in investment." As you can see, in this area, Kalecki's position is very close to that of Keynes, even though the Pole ferociously criticized the Briton.[28] But perhaps one of the major discrepancies lies in Kalecki's interpretation in terms of society and social class. In a worrying reminder of the Great Recession, the Polish economist goes as far as to say that business leaders appreciate production discipline (or "discipline in the factories" as he puts it) and political stability more than profits. "Their class instinct", he adds, "tells them that lasting full employment is unsound from their point of view and that unemployment is an integral part of the 'normal' capitalist system."[29]

Many approaches to economic policy put forth between the outbreak of the crisis in 2008 and the abrupt removal of all stimulus policies in May 2010 are based on premises like the ones seen above, even if those who promote these policies are unaware of it. The same can be said of current investor distrust in sectors of the real economy.

(B) Between 1850 and 2008, recessionary phases in the US resulted in significant falls in profits as a percentage of GDP.[30] The immediate repercussion is that it limits companies' investment capacity, with careful analysis of the period from 1950 to 2008 also revealing a direct correlation between investment and profits. In so-called "normal" circumstances, companies can compensate for lost profits by turning to the credit markets. But when the financial markets are highly volatile, companies have more problems and find it much harder to acquire the capital they need to make investments that during expansionary phases could be better guaranteed by positive results in their operating statements. Thus a vicious circle is formed.

Nevertheless, in the second half of the 1980s and the start of the 21st century there was a marked increase in profits in the financial sector as a proportion of total business profits. The figure rocketed to between 33% and 45%, despite rarely averaging more than 20% at any time since 1950. Put another way, the lion's share of total company profits was not held by the real economy per se but by the parts of the economy directly or indirectly tied to the new scenarios being created by the financial economy. A more detailed view of the data thus suggested that, apart from the instability caused by a highly deregulated financial system, there could be deeper problems that were holding back profits. This meant a situation was likely to develop in which not only finances would need adjusting but also the over-accumulation of investment in areas that were no longer providing the necessary profit for the perpetuation of the economic system. In the early months of 2008, non-financial and non-agricultural US firms already saw quarterly profits slip 24% compared to the same quarter in 2007, so there was already explicit evidence that this was happening. The causes were diverse and included a sharp rise in the prices of raw materials, the rising cost of credit, financial-sector losses (due to revised valuation of banks' balance sheets), and the spread of the crisis around the globe, which essentially affected exporters. None of this was predicted by financial analysts, despite the clear signs that profits were entering a downward cycle, and amazingly they were unaware of key data regarding the over-indebtedness of households and companies and failed to take them into account in their projections.[31]

At this crossroads in the European and global economies, the key parts of the ideological precepts of economic policy began to re-emerge, as I have pointed out. Although this topic seems a world away from the offices of technocrats, it has taken hold of them all. In the context of the economic crisis, the question of economic ideology is more prominent than ever, and a major struggle is taking place whose consequences are of great interest to the social sciences in general and economics in particular.

Notes

1. Interesting analysis of recent economic developments, with emphasis on the economic crisis and social inequalities, can be found in A. Bhaduri, *Development with Dignity: A Case for Full Employment* (New Delhi: National Book Trust, 2005); H. Chang, *Bad Samaritans: Rich Nations, Poor Policies and the Threat to the Developing World* (London: Random House, 2007); R.G. Rajan, *Fault Lines: How Hidden Fractures Still Threaten the World Economy* (Princeton, NJ: Princeton University Press, 2010); G. Duménil and D. Lévy, *Capital Resurgent: Roots of the Neoliberal Revolution* (Cambridge, MA: Harvard University Press, 2007); A. Fumagalli and S. Mezzadra (eds.), *Crisis in the Global Economy: Financial Markets, Social Struggles, and New Political Scenarios* (New York: Semiotexte, 2010); S. Amin et al., *Crisis financiera, económica, sistémica* (Madrid: Maia Ediciones, 2010); R. Tornabell, *El día después de la crisis* (Barcelona: Ariel, 2010); G. de la Dehesa, *La primera gran crisis financiera del siglo XXI* (Madrid: Alianza, 2010); V. Navarro, J. Torres and A. Garzón, *Hay alternativas: Propuestas para crear empleo y bienestar social en España* (Madrid: Sequitur, 2011); P. Martín Aceña (ed.), *Pasado y presente: De la Gran Depresión del siglo XX a la Gran Recesión del siglo XXI* (Bilbao: Fundación BBVA, 2011); A. Oliveres, *Aturem la crisi: Les perversions d'un sistema que és possible canviar* (Barcelona: Angle Editorial, 2011). An analysis that goes beyond what is strictly speaking the sphere of economics and looks at other spheres in which politics, culture and civic action are key factors is T. Judt, *Ill Fares the Land* (New York: Penguin Press, 2010); see also S. Giner, *El futuro del capitalismo* (Barcelona: Península, 2010).
2. See C. Pérez, *Technological Revolutions and Financial Capital: The Dynamics of Bubbles and Golden Ages* (Cheltenham: Edward Elgar, 2002).
3. General overviews of these critical postulates can be found in P. Krugman, *The Conscience of a Liberal* (New York: W.W. Norton, 2007); P. Krugman, *The Return of Depression Economics and the Crisis of 2008* (New York: W.W. Norton, 2009); V. Navarro, J. Torres and A. Garzón.
4. P. Krugman, *The Accidental Theorist and Other Dispatches from the Dismal Science* (New York: W.W. Norton, 1999).
5. D.H. Fischer, *The Great Wave: Price Revolutions and the Rhythm of History* (Oxford: Oxford University Press, 1996). Krugman produced a caustic

critique of such approaches and especially of how so many major corporations elatedly – and pathetically – entertained them, although interestingly they only believed what they wanted to believe, even if it was nonsense (see P. Krugman, *The Accidental Theorist and Other Dispatches from the Dismal Science*, pp. 127–134).

6. R.M. Solow, "How Did Economics Get That Way and What Way Did it Get?", in T. Bender and R.E. *Schorske, American Academic Culture in Transformation: Fifty Years, Four Disciplines* (Princeton, NJ: Princeton University Press, 1998), 57–76, especially p. 74.

7. G.A. Akerlof, W. Dickens and G. Perry, "The Macroeconomics of Low Inflation", *Brookings Papers on Economics Activity*, 1 (1996): 1–76.

8. P. Temin, *Lessons from the Great Depression* (Cambridge, MA: MIT Press, 1989).

9. P. Krugman, "Stable Prices and Fast Growth: Just Say No", *The Economist*, 31 August 1996.

10. In his *opus magnum*, *The Political Economy of Prosperity* (Brookings Institution, 1970), Okun analyses real GDP in the United States in the 1950s, at the start of the Korean War, when unemployment and inflation were very low. He extrapolates national production from those years to the future, taking into account the long-term trend of productivity improvements. Okun thus obtains ceilings for maximum production capacity and full employment for the 1950s and 1960s. He concludes that when GDP changed by 3%, unemployment moved by 1% in the opposite direction. In other words, if unemployment rose 1%, GDP would fall 3%. This approach, known as "Okun's Law", infers that the unemployment elasticity with respect to GDP is 3. This figured remained unchanged throughout the 1970s and 1980s, and only in the 1990s did the elasticity fall to 1.5. See J. Tobin, "Arthur M. Okun (1928–1980)", in S.N. Durlauf, and L.E. Blume (eds.), *The New Palgrave Dictionary of Economics*, 2nd edn. (Basingstoke: Palgrave Macmillan, 2008).

11. S. Bowles, D.M. Gordon and T.E. Weisskopf, *After the Waste Land: A Democratic Economics for the Year 2000* (Armonk, NY: M.E. Sharpe, 1991).

12. J. Stiglitz, *Globalization and its Discontents* (New York: W.W. Norton, 2002).

13. See O. Blanchard, G. Dell'Ariccia and P. Mauro, *Rethinking Macroeconomic Policy*, International Monetary Fund Staff Position Note, 12 February 2010, SPN/10/03.

14. In relation to degrowth, a distinction must be made between well-reasoned arguments such as those found in the monograph of the journal *Ecología Política* (vol. 35, 2008), and in C. Taibo, *En defensa del*

decrecimiento (Madrid: Catarata, 2009), and works aimed at the general public such as S. Latouche, *Le pari de la décroissance* (Paris: Fayard, 2006). http://es.wikipedia.org/wiki/2008 Nicholas Georgescu-Roegen's interpretation is innovative in this respect, both in how he rethinks what "economic man" is and in terms of technology applied to economics – and therefore, to growth – and in turn, the thermodynamic, revolutionary view of economic processes. See the valuable summary in O. Carpintero, *La Bioeconomía de Georgescu-Roegen* (Barcelona: Montesinos, 2006).

15. Especially B. Bernanke, *Essays on the Great Depression* (Princeton, NJ: Princeton University Press, 2000).

16. A similar case to Eccles is the economist George Warren, an agricultural expert who advised President Franklin D. Roosevelt to devalue the dollar to raise commodity prices, effectively forcing the US out of a strict adherence to the rules of the gold standard. The topic was the subject of intense controversy, but the American leader listened to what was the most heterodox position in the 1930s, a time when the myth of the rigid gold standard was considered somewhat of a sacred law. See Ahamed, L., *Lords of Finance: the Bankers who Broke the World* (London: William Heinemann, 2009).

17. It is worth remembering – as the winner of the 2010 Pulitzer Prize Liaquat Ahamed has done – that it was the key decisions of five men between 1920 in 1933 that contributed most to the global economic ruin. The names cannot be ignored: they were the chiefs of the central banks of the United States (Benjamin Strong), Britain (Montagu Norman), France (Émilie Moreau) and Germany (Hjalmar Schacht). The list of illustrious men should include President Hoover, whose contribution was that of inactivity and snap decisions. "The worst is over", he claimed in May 1930, when – to use today's terminology – green shoots began to appear. Two years later, the shoddy housing and living conditions of thousands of Americans had come to be known as Hoovervilles. There was also a marked rise in domestic migration among miserable, impoverished farmers with no property, which was masterfully described in John Steinbeck's enlightening writings and the expressive drawings of the broken cities by Edward Hooper. L. Ahamed.

18. R.B. Reich, "The Great Recession, the Great Recessions and what's ahead", working paper, <http://www.irle.berkeley.edu/conference/2010/materials/reich.pdf>, accessed 17 July 2012.

19. P. Temin; C.P. Kindleberger, *Manias, Panics and Crashes*, 6th edn. (Basingstoke: Palgrave Macmillan, 2011). The amount of literature providing a historical review of crises is immeasurable. Recent works

include: C. Marichal, *Nueva historia de las grandes crisis financieras: Una perspectiva global, 1873–2008* (Barcelona: Debate, 2010); C.M. Reinhart and K.S. Rogoff, *This Time Is Different: Eight Centuries of Financial Folly* (Princeton, NJ: Princeton University Press, 2009); A. Torrero, *La crisis financiera internacional y sus efectos sobre la economía española* (Madrid: Marcial Pons, 2011).

20. See, for instance, A. Costas, "Enseñanzas de la crisis de 2008", in A. Furió et al., *Las crisis a lo largo de la Historia* (Valladolid: Universidad de Valladolid, 2010), 193–237.

21. See S. Hyman, *Marriner S. Eccles: Private Entrepreneur and Public Servant* (Stanford, Calif.: Stanford University Graduate School of Business, 1976), pp. 78–79.

22. These data are based on La Caixa, *Monthly Report*, 331 (2010); Servicio Público de Empleo Estatal; Instituto Nacional de Estadística; and Banco de España.

23. See S. Bentolila et al., *La crisis de la economia española* (Madrid: Fedea, 2010), which provides a critical review of economic policies around the time the recession broke out.

24. According to Marx, the capitalist mode of production has several obstacles to tackle at a certain scale of production, to the extent that it can even stagnate when business profits are hit, but not to satisfy social needs. This distinction is crucial because it focuses attention not on the greater or lesser benefits that government can offer people (which are now so maligned by neo-liberal precepts) and their impact on government budgets, but rather on the profits of business people, who at certain times can tangibly see their production get blocked, drop back or stagnate. At such times, the solution must not be to cut back support for social needs. See M. Dobb, *Capitalismo, crecimiento económico y subdesarrollo* (Barcelona: Oikos Tau, 1975); and K. Marx, *El Capital* (Mexico: Siglo XXI, 1975), especially the third volume.

25. Marx's warning should not cause too much concern, now that his works no longer seem very popular, but he does offer enlightening analyses of the genesis and development of economic crises that have significantly shaped later economists. Interestingly, for instance, the first theory of a centralized socialist economy was developed in 1908 by an Italian economist who was not a socialist, Enrico Barone. Likewise, non-Marxian thinkers like Sidney and Beatrice Webb (they were Fabians, to be precise) predicted a gradual shift from capitalism to socialism brought about by a series of irreversible, cumulative reforms, following the arguments of Marx. Finally, one shouldn't forget the words of the venerable Nobel laureate John Hicks, who said, "Most of those [who wish to fit into place the general course of history] would use the

Marxian categories, or some modified version of them, since there is so little in the way of an alternative version that is available." See E. Hobsbawm, *How to Change the World: Tales of Marx and Marxism* (London: Little, Brown, 2011).

26. See J.E. King, *A History of Post Keynesian Economics since 1936* (Cheltenham: Edward Elgar, 2002).

27. M. Kalecki, "A Macro-Dynamic Theory of Business Cycles", *Econometrica*, 3 (1935): 327–44. J.E. King, pp. 35–37. See also A. Bhaduri, which states that of the various methods used to manage demand, the quickest and most convenient is to step up public spending and take on a financial deficit, a move that would be considered a heresy in the current phase of the Great Recession.

28. The controversy between Keynes and Kalecki was toned down somewhat by Joan Robinson, a direct disciple of the Cambridge economist. Robinson, an economist with a socialist political background, undertook the solid task of melting together Marxist and Keynesian precepts, with Kalecki (who she affectionately called "my Pole") playing a vital influential role. J.E. King. An informative work providing an excellent synthesis of Robinson's positions that is very useful for teaching is J. Robinson and J. Eatwell, *Introduction to Modern Economics* (London: McGraw-Hill, 1973).

29. These ideas, which the *pensée unique* has rejected as obsolete and anachronistic, are still relevant due to the present economic and social situation, well known to recent economic historians. The increase in profits derived from capitalist accumulation is thanks to the fall in production costs, with considerable increments in value described by Paul Baran and Paul Sweezy as the "law of rising surplus", the essence of monopoly capital. This surplus, say the two economists, cannot be absorbed by growing demand or by investment (remember Kalecki's equations), but increasing sales and strong military spending are the only natural outlets when investment is blocked by over-accumulation. There is a marked "Kaleckian" influence on these contributions. P. Baran and P. Sweezy, *Monopoly Capital: An Essay on the American Economic and Social Order* (New York: Monthly Review Press, 1966). Similarly, another heterodox economist, Joseph Steindl, asserts that public spending on weapons between 1940 and the 1970s prevented another dip in the world economy, while in the 1970s crisis unemployment rates were being used to tackle (or as the author put it, as a "weapon" against) inflation, making such a tactic a deliberate, conscious economic policy. See J. Steindl, *Economic Papers 1941–1988* (London: Macmillan, 1990), especially pp. 165–80; and A. Bhaduri.

30. Angus Maddison's works do not present profit-to-GDP series, but they

do include indicators that indirectly link negative economic growth to dips in business activity and economic activity in general. See A. Maddison, *The World Economy: A Millennial Perspective/Historical Statistics* (Paris: OECD Publishing, 1996); A. Maddison, *Contours of the World Economy 1-2030 AD: Essays in Macro-Economic History* (Oxford: Oxford University Press, 2007).

31. All these data were taken from the Federal Reserve, Bloomberg and the Bureau of Economic Analysis. See comments about the data in La Caixa, *Monthly Report*, 325 (2010).

Chapter 4

Economic Ideology

1. The importance of economic history

In May 2011, the former Deputy Assistant Secretary of the US Treasury Brad DeLong, currently an Economics professor at the University of California, Berkeley, wrote an enlightening article about economics as a scientific discipline and its responses to the economic crisis.[1] In a text clearly written for non-specialists, he did not fail to address the difficulties being experienced by a subject that politicians and society as a whole always listen to as if it were a kind of Oracle of Delphi, capable of predicting the future, or at least major future trends, but that has been totally inept in dealing with the depth of this Great Recession. The two thousand economists on the IMF's payroll, armed with their econometric models, their supposedly perfect information, and their impressive collection of masters' degrees and other qualifications awarded by the world's most prestigious universities, continue to indicate in many different reports they published in 2007 and much of 2008 that the economy was not forecast to contract. The same can be said of the World Bank, the ECB and the most venerable economic institutions devoted to economic forecasting.

Academic economists, meanwhile, have been infected by the financial engineering designed by colleagues employed by banks or companies specializing in managing investment funds.[2] These experts have justified the crisis, even devoutly, as if it were a chain of crucial, unshakeable "iron laws". Everything was somehow sanctified by a series of derivatives and regressions that multiplied the chances of raking in hefty profits. And the benefits seem to reach society as a whole, given the high level of access to home ownership and similar assets. The elegant models reinforced the status of their authors to the point that they ignored the realities they were creating so close to home. But these "modellers" have little to teach us. A more accurate understanding of the crisis, covering the historical depths and dimensions, is given by Hyman Minsky, Charles Kindleberger, Barry Eichengreen and George Akerlof.[3] They explain processes, identify the pieces in the complex jigsaw of economics, and avoid the facile simplification of presenting econometrics (which, incidentally, is a very useful tool) abstractly and making the instrument an end in itself, an essential objective placed above the actual events. The authors help explain why so much panic was caused by high-risk mortgage losses, deficiencies in controls of economic hazards in banks with grave dysfunctions and imbalances, the extent of the decline in aggregate demand, the level of inefficiency of the forces responsible for restoring the necessary balances, and the massive debts and deficits taken on by governments to keep afloat the very same people who caused the disaster. But these are all exceptional events. For orthodox economists, the roadmap does not change, even when the results are consistently negative and disturbing. Given the current climate, the words of Bradford DeLong could not be more true: "We need fewer efficient-markets theorists and more people who work on microstructure, limits to arbitrage, and cognitive biases. We need fewer equilibrium business-cycle theorists and more old-fashioned Keynesians and monetarists. We need more monetary historians and historians of economic thought and fewer model-builders. . . . Yet that is not what economics departments are saying nowadays." Economic science's "distraction" is taking a massive toll on all of society. Economics is an empirical discipline, but is also, and most importantly, a social science and is therefore subject to unpredictable changes in people's behaviour.

The ideological, profoundly conservative and orthodox framework has set the agenda for economic policy over the past few years following the crash of major banks since September 2008. All too often people describe the Great Recession as something unknown and completely new, when actually it's not new at all. The economic shocks of the last eighty years show that more advanced economies had become accustomed to seasonal cycles, with contractions caused by the inventory cycle, which I have already referred to as over-accumulation earlier in this book. The events of 2008 also illustrate the consequences of over-indebtedness during the boom phases, which in

the 1930s the great economist Irving Fisher called the "debt deflation crisis". Basically, debt deflation happens when a certain action
(in the current case the sub-prime mortgages crisis) deflates the price
of assets and loan guarantees and has devastating consequences, like
under-capitalization in the banking sector and the credit crunch. One
mustn't forget that this situation occurred when private finances were
tremendously fragile, with severe imbalances (real and/or potential,
depending on each case) in the state treasuries and in the gradual
transfer of these deficits to much of the production sector and to
commercial transactions. Economic policy must not, therefore, be
shaped by the remedies used to tackle seasonal recessions (like, for
instance, the 1991–1993 recession).

At the same time, based on the macroeconomic results available
following the implementation of strict austerity measures and
budgetary discipline, continuing with strong fiscal consolidation
efforts is very ineffective. Here is where the weight of ultra-conservative ideology is most dominant: lax legislation to liberalize the
markets for the private sector, and the dismantling of everything
that affects significant provisions of the welfare state for the public
sector. It is rather curious that the economic crisis started as a result
of high-risk management practices by private consortia and has
ended up infiltrating the public sector, as if ultimately the latter
were directly responsible. There are constant calls for government
debt (and therefore the budget deficit) to be increased, yet there are
no parallel calls focusing on the disproportionate growth of private
debt, caused by banks, insurance companies and government monetary policy.

Not everyone will agree that economic discipline is experiencing
an epistemological crisis. Naturally, it is not necessary to grotesquely
discredit the many contributions economists have made in their
respective specialist areas. As Carmen Reinhart and Kenneth Rogoff[4]
correctly point out, saying that the current crisis is different serves
only to promote the idea that it is impossible to understand, at least
using explanatory insights that were already analysed in previous
recessions, especially the 1929 one. Despite the unique features of
each recession, it is more plausible to find patterns than insur-
mountable differences. To put it concisely, ignoring and forgetting
economic history has hindered efforts to successfully tackle the

current problems. In this respect, one of the first ideological interpretations in the field of economic growth has undoubtedly been the
great debate on industrial development prior to the tertiarization of
economies that were moved forward chronologically in the development of manufacturing.

The factors behind the birth of industrial processes have been the
subject of intense, ongoing controversy, especially since the end of
World War II. Some have suggested the initial stimulus that moved
us towards an industrial society was a direct consequence of the lack
of resources and other ecological effects resulting from the necessity
to meet the needs of an ever-growing population. However, the
Industrial Revolution was not initially about new industries, but the
development of technical innovations in existing industries to make
up for the lack of raw materials brought about by the lack of land.[5]
Several factors should be considered in this regard:

1. The central feature of industrialization was that it represented
a new production method based on huge productivity gains and
economic specialization in all directions. Workers began to con-
verge on major industrial areas, leading to the growth of cities as the
size of the working class increased. Despite this new type of city and
the new dynamic for change that it represented, agricultural society
remained dominant. Workers were incorporated into a division of
labour in which they represented only a small part of total production activity. The new workforce was "free" in the sense that the
labourers were part of a labour market and were closely dependent
on it. Meanwhile, production resources were concentrated in the
hands of a small, industrial, capitalist class. The labourers thus
formed the industrial proletariat, the wage earners – a new social
class.

2. In all industrial revolutions since the British one there has been
a deliberate element of emulation. The textile industry was created
using machinery imported from Britain, or equipment designs
inspired by British machines.[6] To some extent, the pioneering work
in the UK fed the growth of other countries.[7] This allowed followers
of the first stages of industrialization to make the best possible use of
different factors involved in industrial growth and a certain form of
company dependent on finance from banks under government super-

vision. Alexander Gerschenkron has examined this area in depth, emphasizing five specific points:[8]

- 1. The magnitude of the opportunities offered by industrialization depended on the wealth of natural resources available to each country.[9]
- 2. The more technological innovations a country lagging behind can take from a country that is out in front, the greater its industrial growth can be.
- 3. By using more modern techniques, countries that are lagging behind can produce successful industrial processes, especially when they are developed in competition with an advanced country. This explains the tendency for countries that are still in the early stage of industrialization to focus on developing those branches of industry that have seen the most recent and most rapid technological advances.
- 4. In the context of the 19th century, using modern techniques made it necessary to considerably increase the average scale of production plants, so external economies had to be created. For instance, you can't build railways without first opening coal mines. Virtuous circles are formed and the multiplier effects pay off for the sector that initiated the whole process.
- 5. The problems faced by countries lagging behind are not exclusive to them but also affect advanced countries. The 19th-century industrial processes show that policies adopted in areas that are further behind are unlikely to succeed if the main reasons for their backwardness are ignored.

Gerschenkron's vision clearly advocates an accelerated, energy-intensive form of industrialization based on large-scale capital investments (i.e. tons of coal and giant steel and chemical plants) of the kind seen during the Second Industrial Revolution.

However, until the mid-19th century Britain could be considered the only industrialized country.[10] Only in some areas, such as Belgium and western Germany, were there signs of industrialization in the British sense of the word. The UK had no competitors back then, although that began to change in 1870 when new, strong industrial rivals emerged in new sectors using new technologies (steel, chemicals, electricity and combustion engines). The global economy kept growing, although not without some problems:[11] while industrial production increased, growth slowed in more advanced countries, and the spread of industrialization made the struggle for markets even more intense. British exporters were faced with tough competition, especially from Germany and the United States.

The new period that began in 1870 saw the market structure of each country become even more competitive, forcing them to adopt two types of economic policies:

a) Control of competition through the setting up of trusts and cartels. This made the concentration of industrial capital increasingly important.

b) The industrialization of the late 19th century saw growth at the scale of the business unit and the emergence of new financial methods in which banks played a dominant role. New forms were emerging and operating alongside old forms:

- Industrial capitalism was widely promoted in the form of family businesses and companies passed down from one generation to the next.[12] These companies survived, especially in light industry.
- But what changed was when large firms began to be formed and enlarged requiring massive amounts of capital, and taking the form of public limited companies.[13]

All this gave rise to continuous population movements, accompanied by strong urban growth.[14] For instance, in America the urban population grew by 28% between 1880 and 1900, and there were similar patterns in all developed countries. This economic history, synthetically exposed from the perspective of energy constraints, serves to confirm that growth patterns are diverse, shaped by their environments, and that there are no magic formulas to guarantee a certain end result defined by ideological precepts.

One of the key challenges for economic historians is to provide an intelligible, step-by-step explanation as to how a country's wealth was created. While economists analyse the situation to determine the mobility or permanence of indicators, which they examine with the clear aim of predicting the future, economic historians seek out the causes in the immediate or distant past that best explain the present.[15] Identifying lessons from the past to more accurately understand current processes is a relevant strategic approach in economic history, a discipline that has been dubbed by most fellow economists as a kind of big, static laboratory used to validate economic theories. Robert Solow already warned against this fallacious argument, contending that economic history provides the economist with many more tools than simply comparing and contrasting theories.[16] Experience, therefore, is very useful. It is this careful observation of past practices, with the desire to learn from them, that determines actions that sometimes surprise many economic analysts but few economic historians. The current economic events are tied to previous events in which there were economic expansions and crises. People took decisions that affected economic behaviours and social responses and that form part of a collective culture

For a long time, and certainly until the 1930s, economics believed natural resources were the main igniter of a country's development. This meant environmental determinism very often shaped the analyses made on contemporary economic processes. Factors such as abundant coal, water, oil or other inputs urgently needed by industry could bring about industrialization and completely change the direction of society's behaviour patterns, as we have already seen. The United Kingdom, Germany and Belgium are cases in point.[17] The change in the energy model was thus becoming the main exponent of what Karl Polanyi called the "great transformation" and what Lewis Mumford called the transition from an "eotechnic phase" to a "paleotechnic phase".[18] The fossil fuel era, which drastically changed Europe, continued, as did large-scale industrial pollution. Very clearly it was environmental tensions that gave birth to big industry. At the same time, the lack of land increased the relative cost of using animal power, while there were huge quantities of cheap coal to fuel steam engines. So the use of steam developed for environmental reasons. This development was essential so that the problems analysed by David Ricardo did not hold back growth and the tensions identified by Thomas Malthus did not go away.[19] It is becoming increasingly clear that the use of traditional energy during much of the 19th century is one of the fundamental characteristics of industrialization in Great Britain and the United States. Until 1850, the key to the Industrial Revolution was the rise in production, not in the use of steam. Therefore a broader analysis is needed, and the idea that economic growth is so closely tied to technological developments must be reconsidered. The main exponent of this principle is Gerald Gunderson, referring to the United States.[20] Gunderson attacks Rostow's economic growth model and questions it by highlighting how the increase in industrial productivity massively helped growth, but stating that the increase cannot be a defining characteristic. Industrialization was a way of supplying goods for which a market was created by high incomes. Real incomes can also increase thanks to higher production resulting from known methods and existing resources. Where national income comes from is a side issue, because the more pressing issue is to know the quantity of goods and services the income can buy. Consumption is the end of all production and not all production is industrial. Gunderson remarks that in 1800 American income was higher than British income, but if industrialization had been the sole cause of higher income we would have to conclude that the United States was the first industrialized country. But it wasn't. What is true is that the US economy had achieved high growth before industrialization thanks to market expansion resulting from improved transport under traditional systems

To breach the inherent limitations of all organic economies it was essential to establish a new form of capitalism and crucial to find a new source of energy that would improve worker productivity. This would be impossible as long as the only instruments that could be used to process material objects were human muscle and domestic animals. This change in perspective saw an advanced organic economy replaced with one supported by energy extracted through mining. It was not long before people began to believe that manmade, quantifiable capital was the chief instigator of economic development. To this day, people still say that less advanced economies could develop if they could obtain enough capital through their own efforts or with external support. However, these beliefs began to be called into question when people increasingly began to point out that the fundamental causes of economic growth also included non-conventional causes that are completely unrelated to physical capital assets: human strength as a catalyst capable of introducing techniques to improve the efficiency of economic activity.[21]

This is not an entirely new idea. Max Weber identified beliefs, attitudes, value systems and trends that had a favourable influence on generating entrepreneurship and fostered development initiatives.[22] This influence depends not only on being able to identify the appropriate combinations of resources and production factors, but also on achieving the capabilities that are hidden, scattered or simply misused. Such an approach is very different to that made by traditional growth vectors. As indicated by Albert Hirschman, the use of economic resources has repercussions or feedback effects on the supply of those resources. But for some of those resources, such as mineral deposits, the feedback effects disappear: as they are used more, the inputs considered become depleted in the medium or long term. An energy crisis is thus inevitable.[23] A similar pattern occurs for other types of capital, such as monetary capital. As a general rule, capital invested in production processes is easily recovered thanks to the income, and then savings, that it generates. In short, capital investments in a particular company can be rechannelled to become capital for another company that is not necessarily in the same economic sector. But the absence of orthodox growth factors makes these effects hard to spot. The resources increase as they are used each day and are directly related to managing the market, which inevitably makes them difficult to quantify. Only the overall impact they have on the productive fabric reveals the magnitude of the processes these intangibles set off, which are of increasing concern to economists today. That is because these types of resources, which are usually the most scarce in the early stages of development, are those that grow quickest, depending on the magnitude of the feedback and on whether their expansion is limited only by people's learning capacity. The explosion of relations with foreign languages, efficiency in negotiation with all kinds of currencies, and the continual observation – fuelled by the vital need for food and other goods and provisions – of external markets tie the phases of economic growth to fluid extra-regional connections, new networks, trade missions, stimuli for full-blown diasporas and accurate knowledge of the various demands. In other words, economic growth is linked to acquiring a decisive asset: information.[24]

In the late 1950s, the renowned economist E.D. Domar proposed a kind of system for understanding economic growth that has one considerable, difficult-to-refute virtue: its great simplicity.[25] Basically, he says a society has a certain income, part of which it saves and invests. This investment gives rise to new capabilities. In other words (one is aware this is an over-simplification), investment is directly related to savings, which in turn are related to other factors such as technical education (it is important to note I'm not referring to "human capital" as defined by Theodore Schultz in his classical contributions) or knowing how to organize companies structurally.[26] Hirschman used these very direct, synthetic messages to argue that the capacity to invest is acquired and improved through practice. In other words, the economy induces greater capacities, skills and attitudes to improve subsequent development in proportion to the tangible experiences that those attitudes are already infusing in economic players. It is unlikely that any kind of innovation could arise out of nothing.[27] And it is sensible to assume that an economy with a significant number of companies, with different levels of organizational and commercial experiences, will, in turn, acquire a higher number of people with proven skills that have shown their worth in the market than an economy with fewer initiatives. That is the basis for qualitative and quantitative steps towards creating new business activities. In this sense, existing capabilities are the defining asset of an economy that has few natural resources but has shown solid growth patterns in recent decades. Once again, careful analysis of this is not related to unique, irrefutable, unquestionable, dogmatic lines of thought, and certainly not to solutions from a manual.

2. Creating economic objectives

Despite all these theoretical reflections, which have empirical support in the case of European and South American regional economies,[28] I still believe that economies have certain generic objectives that affect the whole of society and that fit the agendas of other experts. These objectives all have one thing in common: the vital role of economic history, which takes into consideration the following points:[29]

1. The urgency to understand a volatile, changing world that is immersed in a systemic crossroads. Globalization has seen the emergence of a world broken into five major economic areas according to Paolo Sylos Labin. First there is Europe, which has stretched eastwards despite initial difficulties due to the lack of convergence between new and more established countries.[30] Second is the ever-expanding Asian region, which as noted in a previous chapter is dominated by two giants, China and India. Both these countries can still be considered part of the so-called Third World, but as we know, both are undoubted leaders in international trade and technical skills, in human capital (especially in fields related to telematics) and in the financial resources they possess from more advanced countries.[31] The third area is Latin America, which has come through tough times, with very difficult political scenarios and lethal public- and private-debt crises, but which has a very clear economic leader in Brazil, which has recently seen massive growth.[32] Fourth is sub-Saharan Africa, which is cut off from northern Africa, whose most symbiotic relations are with the entire Mediterranean basin and whose economic flows are with the energy markets. Black Africa is rich in resources but lacking in political, social and tribal cohesion and plagued by perennial wars. Despite its extreme social poverty, the region has become a fundamental objective of new capitalist expansions, and the origins of this intense greed that wants to profit from all kinds of natural resources are to be found in New York, London, Paris . . . or Beijing.[33] Finally, the fifth major economic area is the United States, a power that is currently in a crisis and is being challenged by the dynamic of this new globalization, but still has latent capabilities in different fields of scientific and applied knowledge.[34]

2. The environment, from a social perspective. Two contradictory observations are often made regarding environmental problems.[35] One is that the environment is specifically a middle-class problem. They say that only people with high incomes can afford to worry about quality of life, and lobby groups concerned for the environment are mainly formed by middle-class people. The other observation is that because the environment is shared by everyone, differences in income and status are irrelevant. They say the environmental crisis signals the end of so-called old-school politics, based on class differences. Both arguments are shaky. First, the fact that poor people can't

afford to buy a good quality of life does not mean they don't want to. The idea that they don't is based on the fallacy that market demands directly reflect consumer desires. It is true that market demand is sustained by consumers. But consumer desires are not always compatible with the resources those consumers have to satisfy their desires. Surveys show that blue-collar workers are just as concerned for having a clean environment as those who are better off. But for poorer people, who must manage scant resources, other needs are a higher priority. Furthermore, in industrialized countries, primarily the middle classes form or join pressure groups, although this does not reflect the scope of environmental concerns in society. But in poorer countries, the environmental-protection movement is primarily led by poor, humble folk, since environmental damage is much greater there. This reveals the flaw in the second argument: it seems untrue that because environmental problems are shared by everyone income differences are irrelevant. Nevertheless, it is true that we all experience effects such as global warming. Pollution shows no respect for residential boundaries either. But not everyone feels the impact of the environmental crisis equally, so the benefits and costs of the environment are distributed unevenly.[36]

3. The ever-worsening problems associated with income disparities. Since the 1980s, inequalities between countries have widened. The ratio of the difference in income between the 20% of the world's population living in the richest countries and the 20% living in the poorest countries was 74:1 in 1997, 60:1 in 1990 and 30:1 in 1960. If we delve further into the past we see that the figures were 11:1 in 1913, 7:1 in 1870 and 3:1 in 1820.[37] By the end of the 1990s, the 20% of the world's population living in countries with the highest income accounted for 86% of global GDP (the 20% living in the countries with the poorest income accounted for only 1%). The rich countries also provided 82% of global exports (vs. 1%), 68% of foreign direct investment (vs. 1%), and 74% of the world's phone lines (vs. 1.5%). Meanwhile, the net wealth of the world's 200 richest people more than doubled in the four years leading up to 1998, surpassing $1 trillion. The assets of the top three multimillionaires is higher than the total GDP of all the least-developed countries and their more than 600 million inhabitants put together. In 1993, just 10 countries were responsible for 84% of global spending on research and for 95% of US patents registered in the last two decades. Despite the efforts made by certain institutions and economists to prove that that inequalities have been reduced in recent years, the data available says quite the opposite, with pessimistic data clearly dominating over more rose-coloured views of the economy and possible advances in poorer parts of the world.

Notes

1. J. Bradford DeLong, "Economics in Crisis", *Project Syndicate*, <http://www.project-syndicate.org/commentary/economics-in-crisis>, accessed 26 August 2012.
2. One of the best documentaries made about the economic crisis is *Inside Job*, directed by Charles H. Ferguson. It challenges some of these academic economists (from such major universities as Harvard, Berkeley and Columbia), who propagated the most intransigent theories favouring deregulation and produced ad hoc glowing reports – for a rather handsome fee – for entities that declared bankruptcy shortly after, including the nation of Iceland.
3. See the bibliography references to the works of Akerlof, Minsky and Kindleberger. Eichengreen, meanwhile, is doing a commendable job bringing the economic and financial data up to date. See B. Eichengreen, "The Slide to Protectionism in the Great Depression: Who Succumbed and Why", working paper 15142, National Bureau of Economic Research (2010); B. Eichengreen, "The Great Recession and the Great Depression: Reflections and Lessons", working paper 593, Central Bank of Chile (2010); and B. Eichengreen and K. O'Rourke, *A Tale of Two Depressions*, VoxEU.org Ebook, 8 March 2010, <http://www.voxeu.org/article/tale-two-depressions-what-do-new-data-tell-us-february-2010-update>, accessed 26 August 2012. http://www.voxeu.org/ A broader approach can be found in B. Eichengreen, *Globalizing Capital: A History of the International Monetary System*, 2nd edn. (Princeton, NJ: Princeton University Press, 2008).
4. C.M. Reinhart and K.S. Rogoff, *This Time Is Different: Eight Centuries of Financial Folly* (Princeton, NJ: Princeton University Press, 2009).
5. Western civilization entered a period of recurring environmental instability between the 16th and 18th centuries. Most countries were faced with an ecological boundary, at the heart of which were tensions over deforestation. Had there not been a drastic increase in the supply of coal, cheap iron, machinery and sundry new chemical products, industrialization could not have overcome the severe organic thresholds of a

technology based on wood, stone, small-scale wind and water power and animal power. Man succeeds in taking control of nature (in the 16th century Francis Bacon said "Man, if we look to final causes, may be regarded as the centre of the World", and in the 18th century Isaac Newton said you have to make nature vomit). The major socio-ecological crisis that sparked this revolution was the wood shortage in England, which was dealt with by massively exploiting the huge fossil fuel deposits hidden under the British soil. That's how the use of coal began to spread in the 17th century. See C. Urdangarin and F. Aldabaldetrecu, *Historia técnica y económica de la máquina herramienta* (San Sebastián: Caja de Ahorros Provincial de Guipúzcoa, 1982), pp. 79 et seq; G. Basalla, *The Evolution of Technology* (Cambridge: Cambridge University Press, 1990), pp. 52 et seq. The success of Thomas Newcomen's steam engine, which condensed steam, enabled water to be extracted from Cornish mines in the early 18th century. But there was one major deficiency: the water cooled the cylinder and when the steam reached the cool area it would only condense in part, resulting in a considerable loss of heat. In James Watt's later design, condensation took place in a separate condensation chamber. This occurred in 1781, at a time when water wheels in rivers were no longer providing enough power, so the steam engine solved the inherent problems of energy.

6. Industrialization was in part the result of earlier growth. Therefore, the distinction between industrialization and growth – one might even speak of a third leg in this conceptual tripod, consisting of development – allows us to dispel the myth of the orthodox theses that emerged out of the British industrial revolution, which some authors have attempted to set in stone and turn into a model for all other countries to follow. See the comments on this in D. Landes, *The Unbound Prometheus: Technological Change and Industrial Development in Western Europe from 1750 to the Present*, 2nd edn. (Cambridge: Cambridge University Press, 2003); T. Kemp, *Historical Patterns of Industrialization*, 2nd edn. (London: Longman, 1993); R. Sylla and G. Toniolo, *Patterns of European Industrialization. The Nineteenth Century* (London: Routledge, 1993).

7. The Scandinavian countries provided a different, clearly successful industrialization pattern, which also justified the subsequent economic and social developments. For an introduction, see T. Kjærgaard, *The Danish Revolution, 1500–1800: An Ecohistorical Interpretation* (Cambridge: Cambridge University Press, 1994); L. Jörberg, "Structural Change and Economic Growth: Sweden in the 19th Century", P.K. O'Brien (ed.), *The Industrial Revolutions: The*

Industrial Revolution in Europe, II (Oxford: Blackwell, 1994), 412–54. S. Heikkinen and R. Hjerppe, "The Growth of Finnish Industry in 1860–1913: Causes and Linkages", in P.K. O'Brien (ed.), *The Industrial Revolutions: The Industrial Revolution in Europe*, II (Oxford: Blackwell, 1994), 363–80. F. Hodne, "Growth in a Dual Economy: The Norwegian Experience, 1814–1914", in P.K. O'Brien (ed.), *The Industrial Revolutions: The Industrial Revolution in Europe*, XVI (Oxford: Blackwell, 1994), 381–410.

8. See A. Gerschenkron, *Economic Backwardness in Historical Perspective: A Book of Essays* (Cambridge, MA: Belknap Press of Harvard University Press, 1962).

9. However, many countries had hardly any coal, making it more expensive to run the steam engines, with many industries opting instead for water power. This happened in many parts of the United States that played an important role in key industrial sectors, while in Alpine regions, where vast quantities of water regularly gush down the mountains, there was a firm commitment to use water power in the Swiss textile industry, northern Italy and southern Germany. France had scarce coal resources, so it made a firm decision to promote water power, which can be considered the energy of the first industrial revolution in France, with water wheels and turbines operating at most manufacturing facilities until almost 1860. Water provided between two thirds and three quarters of total power, but by 1880, steam power had become as important as water power. France's delay in switching to steam power has a simple explanation: water power was considered free and close to home, while steam power was expensive and made businesses dependent upon external sources, thus making industry more vulnerable. See D. Woronoff, *Histoire de l'industrie en France* (Paris: Seuil, 1998), pp. 204 et seq.

10. T. Kemp, pp. 155–156.

11. The crisis that affected western countries between 1870 and the end of the 19th century was overcome thanks to a new leap forward in the process of capital accumulation. Replacing human and animal energy with mechanical energy was once again the solution, with coal and steam use being stepped up. Between 1873 and 1895 coal consumption quadrupled in America, tripled in Germany and England and doubled in France. By the end of the 19th century, the main fuel used was coal (70%), followed by wood (27%) and gas, water power and oil (3%). To shake off the constraints on all organic economies, countries had to be capitalist not only in the conventional sense of the word, but also in the sense of a gradual shift to raw materials being extracted from mineral reserves rather than from annual flows of agricultural produc-

tion. See G. Feliu and C. Sudrià, *Introducció a la història econòmica mundial* (Universitat de València–Universitat de Barcelona, 2006), pp. 241–69.

12. D. Landes, *Dinastías: Fortunas y desdichas de las grandes familias de negocios* (Barcelona: Crítica, 2006). Landes's vision, which is of great interest, essentially highlights the family side of large companies around the world, championing this direct, close-to-home control of business developments by the saga, the dynasty.

13. A.D. Chandler, *The Visible Hand: The Managerial Revolution in American Business* (Cambridge, MA: Harvard University Press, 1977). This is a very different perspective from that of Landes. Chandler believes the professionalization of company management explains the triumph of large-scale American consortia, with the eruption of new figures linked to business management who did not belong to family groups.

14. Part of Europe's fast-growing population (those unable to find work opportunities in their native regions) emigrated to other continents. Between 1821 and 1915, 43.6 million people left Europe. The countries producing the largest numbers of emigrants were the United Kingdom, Germany, Austria-Hungary, Italy, Spain and Portugal, and other southern and eastern European countries. Almost all rural areas from which people emigrated were regions where land ownership consisted mainly of large estates. Very few left France, however. Nearly 8 million Asians, mainly from India and China, also went through Europe on their way to the New World. The demographic transition commenced as the death rate began to decline during the first half of the 19th century, with many European countries not seeing a corresponding decline in the birth rate until the early 20th century, or even later, resulting in a huge rise in the European population. By 1920, Europe was the home to 26.8% of the world's population, the highest percentage in its history. See K. Bade, *Migration in European History* (Oxford: Blackwell, 2003).

15. The cliometrician Deirdre C. McCloskey has said that predictions are impossible in economics. With ironic acidity, she says "the industry of making economic predictions, which includes universities, earns only normal returns", never rising yields, despite how society reveres professional economists who make predictions – generally failed predictions – about interest rates. See D.N. McCloskey, "The Rhetoric of Economics", *Journal of Economic Literature*, 21/2 (1983): 481–517.

16. R.M. Solow, "Economics: Is Something Missing?", in W.N. Parker (ed.), *Economic History and the Modern Economist* (Oxford: Basil Blackwell, 1986), especially pp. 28–29.

17. Nevertheless, Paul Krugman believes that natural resources are not such a decisive factor in determining where industrialization takes

place. His view of the genesis of the industrial belt in the north-east of the United States is more in line with the Marshallian ideas of creating industrial atmospheres rather than with those who believe in the need for greater access to raw materials. Geographical concentration of industry, he says, is actually a product of demand externalities, increasing returns and transport costs. See P. Krugman, *Geography and Trade* (Cambridge, MA: MIT Press, 1991). The spatial aspects of economics have been strengthened by new publications that have revived Alfred Marshall's external economies: M. Fujita, P. Krugman and A.J. Venables, *The Spatial Economy: Cities, Regions, and International Trade* (Cambridge, MA: Massachusetts Institute of Technology, 2000), pp. 28 et seq.

18. The key works are K. Polanyi, *The Great Transformation: The Political and Economic Origins of our Time* (Boston, , MA: Beacon Press, 2001); and L. Mumford, *Technics and Civilization* (Chicago: University of Chicago Press, 2010). Note that these books were first published in 1944 and 1930 respectively.

19. C. Napoleoni, *Smith, Ricardo, Marx: Observations on the History of Economic Thought* (Oxford: Basil Blackwell, 1975).

20. G. Gunderson, *A New Economic History of America* (New York: McGraw-Hill, 1976).

21. See A.O. Hirschman, *The Strategy of Economic Development* (New Haven, CT: Yale University Press, 1958). The author says economic growth is unbalanced and development planning is effective when it combines efforts in key industries, which must link up with other industries on both sides. Hirschman's book managed to separate development economics as a discipline related to the growth trajectories of less-developed countries from the theory that growth is linked to abstract characteristics of mathematical models. For more about this relatively unknown economist see L. Meldolesi, *Discovering the Possible: The Surprising World of Albert O. Hirschman* (London: University of Notre Dame Press, c. 1995); See M.S. McPherson, "Hirschman, Albert Otto (born 1915)", in S.N. Durlauf, and L.E. Blume (eds.), *The New Palgrave Dictionary of Economics*, 2nd edn. (Basingstoke: Palgrave Macmillan, 2008); M. Blaug, *Great Economists since Keynes* (Cheltenham: Edward Elgar, 1998).

22. M. Weber, *General Economic History* (Mineola, TX: Dover Publications, 2003).

23. This conclusion, which identifies raw materials as scarce, and therefore exhaustible, has led to a whole series of contributions in the fields of ecological economics and the history of ecological economics, which are linked to sustainable development theory. For an excellent summary

see J. Martínez Alier and J. Roca Jusmet, *Economía ecológica y política ambiental* (Mexico: Fondo de Cultura Económica, 2006), pp. 294–363; S. Álvarez and O. Carpintero (eds.), *Economía ecológica: reflexiones y perspectivas* (Madrid: Círculo de Bellas Artes, 2009).

24. See some historical examples in W.M. Reddy, *The Rise of Market Culture: The Textile Trade and French Society, 1750–1900* (Cambridge: Cambridge University Press, 1987); and S. Pollard, *Marginal Europe: The Contribution of Marginal Lands since the Middle Ages* (Oxford: Oxford University Press, Clarendon Press, 1997).

25. See M.A. Galindo and G. Malgesini, "Crecimiento económico: Principales teorías desde Keynes", *Cuadernos*, 25 (1993): 61–8. It is important to note that post-Keynesian growth models proposed by R.F. Harrod and E.D. Domar did not consider technological change to be a growth factor, while the neo-classical models proposed by Solow and Abramovitz emphasize the importance of technical progress as an exogenous variable with its own, independent economics laws. In this regard, Nathan Rosenberg has highlighted the current tendency in economics to treat technological change as a kind of "black box" based on a series of assumptions that have confused the issue, rather than clarifying it. N. Rosenberg, *Inside the Black Box: Technology and Economics* (Cambridge: Cambridge University Press, 1982).

26. The human capital theory was proposed by Schultz following a research programme based around the idea that people naturally spend on themselves in very different ways, not only searching for "utility" in the present, but also pursuing future monetary and non-monetary outputs. Schultz argues that people voluntarily purchase education and additional professional training, spend time finding a job that is most challenging to them rather than accepting the first offer they get, and even prefer working for lower wages if the potential earnings are high. See T. Schultz, "Education and Economic Growth", in N. Henry, *Social Forces Influencing American Education* (Chicago: University of Chicago Press, 1961); T. Schultz, *Investing in People: The Economics of Population Quality* (Berkeley, CA: University of California Press, 1981). Regarding new theories on endogenous growth, essential reading includes: P. Romer, "Increasing returns and long-run growth", *Journal of Political Economy*, 94 (1986): 1002–37; P. Romer, "Human Capital and Growth: Theory and Evidence", NBER working paper 3173, <http://www.nber.org/papers/w3173>, accessed 17 July 2012; A.R. Lucas, "On the Mechanics of Economic Development", *Journal of Monetary Economics*, 22 (1988): 3–42.

27. Jason Schumpeter has had a decisive influence in shaping theories on innovation from the perspective of technology. But Schumpeter's focus

is more on major innovations, leaving aside minor innovations such as the gradual introduction of other processes and products, in which learning, copying and disseminating are central to economic growth. See S. López, "De exploración con Schumpeter", in S. López and J.M. Valdaliso (eds.), *¿Que inventen ellos? Tecnología, empresa y cambio económico en la España contemporánea* (Madrid: Alianza, 1997), 93–4.

28. For Spain, an overview broken down by region is found in E. Llopis et al., *Historia económica regional de España* (Barcelona: Crítica, 2003). For Italy, where the study of regional economics has been greatly developed, there is an unending amount of literature, but as an introduction see L. Cafagna, *Dualismo e sviluppo nella Storia d'Italia* (Venice: Marsilio, 1989). A general perspective is found in R. Capello, "La economía regional tras cincuenta años: desarrollos técnicos recientes y desafíos futuros", *Investigaciones Regionales*, 9 (2006): 171–94.

29. See P. Sylos Labini, *Torniamo ai classici: Produttività del lavoro, progresso tecnico e sviluppo economico* (Bari: Laterza, 2005); J. Rifkin, *The Third Industrial Revolution: How Lateral Power is Transforming Energy, the Economy, and the World* (New York: Palgrave Macmillan, 2011). A similar perspective focusing on the Balearic Islands is found in C. Manera, *L'eixam i les abelles: Per un nou model de creixement a les Illes Balears* (Barcelona: Publicacions de l'Abadia de Montserrat, 2009).

30. J. Fontana, *Europa ante el espejo* (Barcelona: Crítica, 1994); A. Alesina and F. Giavazzi, *El futuro de Europa. Reforma o declive* (Barcelona: Antoni Bosch Editor, 2009).

31. G. Arrighi, *Adam Smith in Beijing: Lineages of the Twenty-First Century* (London: Verso, 2007); F. Lemoine, *L'économie de la Chine* (Paris: La Découverte, 2003); M. Renard, *China and its Regions: Economic Growth and Reform in Chinese Provinces* (Edward Elgar: Cheltenham, 2002); J. Studwell, *The China Dream: The Elusive Quest for the Greatest Untapped Market on Earth* (London: Profile Books, 2002). Highly innovative views of the economic growth in today's emerging countries, from a historical perspective, can be found in R.B. Marks, *The Origins of the Modern World: Fate and Fortune in the Rise of the West*, rev. and updated edn. (Lanham, Md.: Rowman & Littlefield, 2007), especially pp. 123 et seq.; D. Landes, *The Wealth and Poverty of Nations: Why Some Are So Rich and Some So Poor* (New York: W.W. Norton, 1998), pp. 22 et seq.;

32. C. Marichal, *A Century of Debt Crises in Latin America: From Independence to the Great Depression, 1820–1930* (Princeton, NJ: Princeton University Press, 1989); C. Marichal, *Latinoamérica y España* (Madrid: Marcial Pons, 2009).

33. J. Fontana, "El triunfo del capitalismo realmente existente", *Claves de Razón Práctica*, 217 (2011): 10–16; For the new investment of global

powers in Africa, see A. Bodomo, *La globalización de las inversiones en África* (Madrid: Catarata, 2011).

34. On the importance of the United States in this field, see the relevant chapters in J. Mokyr, *The Gifts of Athena: Historical Origins of the Knowledge Economy* (Princeton, NJ: Princeton University Press, 2002); J. Fontana, *Por el bien del imperio: Una historia del mundo desde 1945* (Barcelona: Pasado y Presente, 2011), pp. 833–75.

35. I am following the arguments in M. Jacobs, *The Green Economy: Environment, Sustainable Development and the Politics of the Future* (Concord, MA: Pluto Press, 1991).

36. An essential reference on this point is J.M. Naredo, *Raíces económicas del deterioro ecológico y social: Más allá de los dogmas* (Madrid: Siglo XXI, 2006).

37. The figures are taken from the United Nations Development Programme (UNDP) reports for different years. Historical data for income are found in A. Maddison, *The World Economy: A Millennial Perspective/Historical Statistics* (Paris: OECD Publishing, 1996).

Chapter 5

The Instability of Capitalism

1. The collapse of the system

Capitalism is unstable. It is necessary to say this, because too often the official discourse makes people believe that the system is balanced, with few internal contradictions. Capitalism regularly causes crises, which are great or small depending on their causes (financial, production, trade) and especially on the accumulation process that affects specific production sectors. In short, crises represent under-utilization of production capacities and the squandering of physical and human resources. The measures undertaken to tackle these crises must not look only at "technical" considerations, since they prioritize adjusting indicators such as government debt and deficit, which have major repercussions on government accounts. Crises also have major social repercussions, so we must devise tools that not only make government more efficient, but also ensure an essential aspect is taken into account when government policies are deployed: higher income. Wanting to sell across-the-board tax cuts is a short-sighted attitude. Quite the opposite needs to be done. Governments need to increase their ability to bring in revenue and throw the Laffer curve onto the scrapheap to maintain and consolidate public services that have characterized the welfare state in Europe. At the very least, this is an alternative ideology, more deeply rooted in the principles of social democracy, which has helped reinforce historical feats achieved by the working class. The data regarding this ideology are highly illustrative: according to Eurostat, in 2010 the tax burden in the eurozone reached 44.6% of GDP, while in Spain, for example, it reached 36.3%.[1] This partly explains the difference between countries in the position of government finances and disparities in the provision of all kinds of public services. Demonizing taxes is highly irresponsible in times of crisis. What needs doing is to discuss taxes in a more focused way, since not all taxes can be adjusted. In the not-too-distant future we will probably see a review of the tax basket, with it becoming increasingly fashionable to "fine-tune" the tax burden (for example, introducing and increasing "green" taxes) and lower other taxes that can be reduced. Contracting taxation is not a good way of meeting the challenges that are arising from the crisis, the challenges that the ideology of economics highlights the most, the most direct challenges: identifying the state's proper role in the economy and basic public services.

One interventionist view of economic development that is very much in tune with this idea and has been gaining ground as an unassailable *pensée unique* is that if certain pre-established phases are completed it will inevitably lead to success (this is the idea behind the present policies of austerity and a drastic reduction in the government deficit).[2] But this is a strange view when economic science as a discipline has failed so drastically, especially in accurately detecting and analysing the economic crisis. At the same time, the remedies that have been used since May 2010 have merely confirmed the resounding collapse of global macroeconomics, with very few exceptions. The ability of governments to trip over the same obstacles and make the same mistakes gets rather frustrating and warnings have become useless. Those at the top of the international economics hierarchy are stuck in a "Hoover phase" (named after the American president who led the first few years of the 1930s Great Depression, creating much outcry), that is, a phase with rigid, orthodox protocol and little permeability in which debt and deficit control are the two mainstays of all economic policy. But it was the arrival of the "Roosevelt phase" (the president after Hoover ignored everything the gold-standardist academics and advisers were telling him and applied strategies to stimulate aggregate demand rather than strict, tough austerity measures) that made possible a feasible, real end to the worst crisis known by capitalism. Moreover, there are other factors, which are essential from a production standpoint, that must be taken into consideration:

1. There is no clear candidate to take over the current Technological Revolution. If we accept that technological revolutions have brought about technical, organizational, cultural and

geographical changes and have determined key changes in the international economy (linked to new products, and therefore new market niches), there do not seem to be any substitution processes right now. In other words, capital has been directed more towards starting up and stimulating speculative activities (capital that invests in capital), rather than stimulating new production areas, which in turn will help to prolong the accumulation process.[3] Waves of innovation focused on technology for the general public take place every 50–60 years according to Kondratieff's thesis. Recent innovations have shortened the wavelength to 30 years. It would not be rash to expect future innovations to shrink this timespan further. However, the priority area of investment of pension funds and sovereign wealth funds (i.e. what the media daily refer to as the "markets") is government debt. The performance of government debt is limited but safe, although speculation pushes up the cost of some countries' products, which are considered more risky. The differentials with Germany – the famous risk "premiums" – have become the major indicator of contrast to quantify the level of distrust towards a particular country.

2. The so-called "markets" invest more in speculation than in the real economy. It is therefore rather subversive to explain why they do not invest in economic activities and areas that are potentially profitable, such as environment-related areas and the battle against climate change, in which there are also potentially high profits, undoubtedly higher than certain operations that are limited to the sphere of finance. On this point there is a political consensus (though also much hypocrisy, as seen in the resolutions passed by climate-change summits) expressed through unequivocal declarations issued by the White House or European Commissioners and through meticulous contributions from a range of scientific fields.[4] But this consensus does not translate into plausible, ambitious investment programmes that affect not only energy, but also production – in other words, the way of doing things, which is what will enable a surer, more forceful leap forward. However, in many OECD economies there are clearly new activities involving different sectors, such as the digital, environmental and cultural sectors. There are even changes in the industrial sector, which combines goods and manufactured products with a high added value and services (known as "manu-services").[5]

3. There are new investment opportunities that are attractive to capital and good for the planet's sustainability, such as renewable energies and information and communication technologies (ICTs), as has been widely publicized.[6] However, a few considerations are necessary:

- Renewable energies have a limited use. Although they can be used to maintain a kind of status quo, they do not solve the core energy problem, since current technology requires energy to be used to produce renewable energy. Investment must target production processes that improve energy effectiveness and efficiency (and as a result, overall effectiveness and efficiency), so the main priority must be exergy, i.e. energy that can do useful work. This is how we get technological applications that consume less of all kinds of inputs and produce less toxic waste, and knowledge-economy activities, whether linked to environmental engineering or to physicochemical developments in thermodynamics.[7] Many steps forward have been taken in these directions, but there is still very strong opposition to diversifying energy sources and production processes despite the difficult situation and the challenges posed by the end of fossil fuels as a cheap, accessible energy source.[8]

- ICTs are also presented as a set of decisive activities to change growth models. A major debate is taking place over this, involving a broad spectrum of professionals, and this has key ramifications throughout what we call the "knowledge economy" (that is, the quaternary sector of the economy).[9] But while the importance of ICTs cannot be denied and can be demonstrated with data in hand, they cannot be considered to automatically produce fast, radical changes to forms of growth. In fact, the demographic changes in developed countries, where the population is clearly ageing, means those countries will need a bigger workforce in the future rather than widespread use of technology if they want to preserve the pillars of the welfare state. Technologies will be vital to sort and analyse situations, but direct work will be related not to ICTs but to the deployment of activities that are more quinary: labour-intensive care for the elderly, including care by their families.

Protectionist social and environmental policies will be urgently needed, which will boost employment capacity.

4. Despite the current budgetary difficulties and the obsession with reducing the deficit by limiting the capabilities of the public sector, consumer demand for services like education, health and geriatric care is expected to continue its upward trend and to increase in more and more advanced segments, requiring open competition for highly qualified staff and other skilled staff. In other words, people will need to be cared for by people, not by machines or precision technology. This profoundly important issue is part of the ongoing debate on how services should be developed in mature societies, bearing in mind that this tertiary sector is so much vaster and more complex than one could have imagined just thirty years ago. There is a huge contrast here, with very different qualifications and wide-ranging levels of productivity that are difficult to measure. It is therefore essential that we consider changing the size of the welfare state and reflect on what areas need expanding in response to population and life-expectancy changes and migratory movements.[10]

5. There are limits to what austerity measures should cover. Those that affect people's welfare should not be introduced.[11] The severe economic austerity measures have led to a clearly thrifty approach to government spending, while the same has occurred in the private sector of the economy. Critics of public investment point out that too often there are no cost-benefit analyses before investment is carried out, and they claim private companies are a model of efficiency in this respect. However, if the dominant ideology becomes blind to reality, with government having to save as much money as possible while the private sector is struggling to keep afloat, the outcome seems pretty obvious: "bad" investments (in Hayek's terms) are liquidated, but economic activities, and therefore also the formation of income, are destroyed too (according to the precepts of Keynes). Everyone will end up too poor to save up money. It also has another down side: deep indiscriminate cuts can worsen the debt problem. With austerity measures stemming growth capacity and the private sector still suffering from the economic collapse, there will be too many debts that are hard to repay, which the so-called markets will find hard to digest. And nobody can calculate or predict when the financial bottleneck will end. The upshot of it all is a drastic reduction in aggregate demand, with even the IMF indicating that austerity and fiscal-consolidation measures in times of crisis are tantamount to suicide.[12]

2. The way out of unleashed capitalism

Arguments are given that suggest areas of action:

1. Very difficult times lie ahead. Global capitalism is currently focused more on tightening its grip on strict market relations than on cementing democracy, expanding education or improving opportunities for the most vulnerable members of society. It is not enough simply to defend the globalization of markets. We must go beyond these priorities that emanate from economic and political powers. Global commercial interests usually have a clear preference for working in ordered, well-organized autocracies rather than in activist democracies. As the Nobel economics laureate Amartya Sen, the financier George Soros, the linguist Raffaele Simone and the writer Hans Magnus Enzensberger explain from very different angles, global capitalism has a regressive influence on the equitable development of society. Globalization in the sense of cooperation, however, can bring about market equilibrating processes, which are not necessarily bad news.[13] On this question, the more academic economists have put forward some interesting lines of thought. The Nobel economics laureate, expert in game theory and distinguished mathematician John F. Nash, Jr., who even inspired a film about his life, said way back in 1950 that the key is not whether a particular agreement is better for everyone than a total absence of cooperation but rather whether the resulting benefits are distributed fairly. The best form of action is in choosing between options, rather than adopting unidirectional approaches.[14]

2. Given these possibilities to choose and the context of widespread globalization, energy is a key challenge. This is where the price mechanism can be most useful. New tax schemes can be deployed, such as carbon taxes combined with carbon "credits", or more taxes that take into account the inherent externalities of economic activities, such as tax policies for service economies (for instance, tourism

bed taxes). The energy problem has been put to one side, overshadowed by the domination of financial macroeconomics. Rifkin and Soros have both said this from their conservative platforms. But for years ecological and environmental economists and social scientists have been preaching in the midst of an academic desert maintained by the apprehension and scepticism towards approaches that consider the more biological, much more correct side of economics, a side that is more open to the outside and more holistic.[15] The energy crisis can thus be interpreted as the other side of globalization. The way out of the crossroads formed by the gradual depletion of cheap oil and coal will foster different scenarios that, once again, will depend on the choices made and the capacity to make the right choices based on the principles of justice and fairness for current and future generations.

3. There is definitely a way out of the crisis. But I'm sceptical as to whether that way out would benefit society if the orthodox measures that are taking over government agendas are implemented. Blatant pessimism has seeped into public opinion, shaking consumers and investors, keeping them away from productive activities and destroying any prospects for the future. However, going all the way back to the Middle Ages, history is littered with major, intense, systemic economic crises. This may be but a short portion of history, yet it is too long for economists to deal with. Yet it is a period that provides lessons that should be heeded so that wiser actions are taken in the present. In all the crises the necessary means to get back on the right track and head towards a recovery have always been found. The same will surely happen with the Great Recession. Among other reasons, it is no different from other crises of this magnitude, but has simply become more widely known, practically in real time, thanks to globalization, with the media observing the depths and consequences of the crisis as events unfold. One of the aspects the flood of information has revealed is obliviousness, dissipation and improvisation. In other words, against a backdrop of panic, political and economic leaders with the potential to transform the existing roadmap do not have clear lines of action. We must dispel the myth so often propagated that those responsible for economic policy have access to perfectly accurate information and therefore know the changes that are on the horizon. These myths lead people to believe that economists work on the basis of equilibrium, when in fact capitalism is essentially unbalanced and unbalancing. It is therefore very hard to predict changes accurately on the basis of rosy assumptions. The crisis can be precisely this: reviewing, rethinking, destroying, radical change . . . but also new opportunities that are not always easy to spot and embark upon in such turbulent times.

It is essential that we analyse whether the stimulus measures introduced between July 2008 and early 2010 bore fruit. We must also do the same checks for the fiscal-consolidation measures introduced between May 2010 and the end of 2011. For the reasons I have explained in this book, I believe the latter measures have been bad for the economy, since we have slipped back into depression, even though in late 2009 there were signs of a slight recovery. Past experiences ought therefore to show that three lines of action are vital, given the instability in the crisis:

a) The ECB should become the lender of last resort – a solvent institution able to stem or even stop speculative attacks against sovereign debt.

b) The ECB should be able to increase the money supply, given the underlying contained inflation in the EU. This would mirror the action taken at different times by the Federal Reserve, the Bank of England and the Bank of Japan, the central institutions of countries with the real possibility of printing more money.

c) Speculative capital flows should be recorded, because as explained earlier in this book, the costs claimed from the financial system that was partly, albeit not solely, responsible for the economic collapse are almost zero. This must be properly addressed as soon as possible. Financial losses should not all be lumbered onto the working and middle classes. Quotas are needed to correctly establish the economic reality and the procedures undertaken by leaders and speculators motivated only by a financial greed that is a far cry from the realities of economics.

4. After the crisis, many unemployed people will struggle to find jobs. Growth is likely to move back above 2%, depending on the performance of the sectors that set the tone for economic growth (goods exports, a recovery of the construction sector, the development of tourism, a resumption of high-tech activity, etc.). Nevertheless, the new opportunities will not be able to find jobs for the many unskilled unemployed people who used to work in labour-intensive production processes – the very people who are the direct, lethal consequence of the Great Recession. This harsh reality will be particularly felt by economies with structural unemployment rates exceeding 10%, where it will become a social problem requiring strong responses from government. The market alone will not solve such a deep, difficult problem. In the interest of basic fairness, stimuli will be urgently required to ensure society does not become too unbalanced. It was social benefits introduced following the 1929 and 1973 crises that eased the negative externalities resulting from the recessions. But this requires stepping up public spending in the area of direct investment to create jobs and boost private-sector activity and in areas that will maintain or even increase current spending, which is considered another form of investment, since it deals with consolidating the welfare state. Clearly the welfare state can be developed if the discourse on government debt and deficit is in line with factors a), b) and c) described in section 3 above.

5. Given what I have discussed, it is not unreasonable to hypothesize about the possible consequences if the countries struggling most leave the euro. Those countries are Spain, Portugal, Greece and even Italy. By exiting the single currency they would have the power to devalue their currency and recover their central banks so they can draw up a monetary and fiscal policy that is more in line with their national interests. This hypothesis is based on a fundamental premise: according to the data presented in this book, Germany has been the country that has benefitted most from monetary union, based on official figures on changes in the balance of payments and economic growth. It is therefore unacceptable to propagate this virulently orthodox economic Lutheranism, which always frowns suspiciously on the south, repeating the dubious idea that the south has lived beyond its means. As I have explained, the German and French financial systems are not blameless and have committed actions that explain some of the investment booms in the Iberian peninsula. But the determining factor in the multi-speed Europe is the absence of a clear German leadership as the driving force behind the European economy. Germany has acted too locally, too domestically, and has failed to take the whole of the eurozone into account in terms of stimulating growth and regulating and balancing government finances.

6. Governments seem anxious about the power of the markets, especially since capital can be moved with lightning speed. Meanwhile, fiscal policies to combat unemployment, whether by taking on deficits or raising tax on the rich, are frowned upon by the financial markets, which warn that such policies would cause prices to rebound, so governments reject such policies. People seem to have accepted the notion that a certain level of unemployment is acceptable, and is justified by inflationary control. But a word of warning is necessary: I believe it is becoming increasingly clear, based on macroeconomic variables for 2008–11, that this results in a drop in demand, and even a big rise in bank liabilities. The drop in demand – a factor being ignored – is because wage cuts reduce consumption, as do increases in work production due to job cuts.[16] In this respect, current economic policies seek to reduce the role of the state, assuming the market works better. The simple, rigid ideas are based on a very clear ideological line: that the markets seldom fail, and it is the markets, through private-sector initiatives, that provide jobs. Government policies need only create the necessary context for businesses to increase profitability and thus provide enough jobs.

7. If the remedies imposed during the crisis continue, there will most likely be years of economic slowdown. However, in addition to technical measures based on a different type of economic policy, profound reflections that steer clear of demagogy and simple formulas are becoming more prominent than ever. Economists cannot churn out the same old trite, often empty phrases repeated over and over by certain institutions, who so often claim to be much more trustworthy than is borne out by economic history, where their ideas have already worn thin. New approaches, arguments, narratives and conceptual frameworks are needed, not the ones we've heard before. The new ideas must create the potential to protect everything people worked so hard to achieve, accomplish and benefit from in the past, including universal education and health care, social services, and the idea that everything that is public belongs to us all and can protect us against the dysfunctions of markets, which should be free, but should also be subject to the appropriate regulations to prevent abuse by those who hold the most symmetrical, most compact, most privileged information. As Eric Hobsbawm says, the world needs to return to the values of the Enlightenment to tackle the future, since in this new century peace is still a distant goal and endemic threats will continue in much of the world.[17]

We need clear, strong, solid leadership that does not waver, except when necessary to recover the strength to boost economic action and reorient it towards scenarios that stimulate investment, dispel the myths surrounding financial instruments and indicators (deficit, debt) and are related to the cycles in economic dynamics. The scenarios should also foster the demand capacity of businesses and households in a way that clearly protects environmental assets and therefore promotes responsible consumption. The citizens of the old continent expect their leaders to protect them from the destruction of wealth that has violently attacked the most vulnerable levels of society, with increasingly perceptible negative consequences for the middle and poorer classes. The public, which feels uneasy at having been affected by the crisis, also needs clear signs of confidence. A massive task lies ahead for European social democracy. New roadmaps are needed that fully take into consideration the challenges posed by environmental imbalances, climate change and attacks on the environment resulting from deregulated economic-growth policies. Old axioms that are definitely not obsolete must also return and flourish, including social justice, solidarity and maintaining the welfare state – ideas originated, of course, by the Enlightenment. New agendas must also be taken aboard that are tangibly concerned for senior citizens, children's living conditions and improving the role of women in the labour and professional markets. We therefore need a reformed, shared social welfare supported by effective, efficient government bodies and progressive fiscal policies. Crises are, after all, opportunities to redesign routines and standards that are supposedly set in stone, continuing with this disruptive idea of transformation. As the great Albert Einstein once said (in a supremely subversive statement):

All crises bring progress. It is in crisis that inventiveness, discoveries and big strategies are born. He who overcomes crisis, overcomes himself. The real crisis is that of incompetence. Without crisis, there are no challenges. You have to work hard to quash the only crisis that is a threat: the tragedy of not wanting to fight to overcome it.

Notes

1. See D. Alonso et al., *Evolución del sistema fiscal español: 1978–2010* (Madrid: Instituto de Estudios Fiscales, 2011).
2. This *pensée unique* was created by institutions such as the Mont Pelerin Society founded by Friedrich Hayek in 1947. Similarly, the Saint-Simon Foundation was established in France, the Institute of Economic Affairs in Britain and the Heritage Foundation in the United States. From these powerful think tanks arose theories that have permeated the economic, social, cultural and scientific thinking of the far right across the world, with theories that scoff at the effects of climate change, reject Darwinism and extol all creationist theories, or claim that poverty is the result of low intelligence or race. Their success is remarkable: by the end of 2010, a survey in the US revealed that 78% of Americans did not trust the theory of evolution, while 40% were convinced that God created the world 10,000 years ago, with humans living for many years alongside the dinosaurs. See J. Fontana, *Por el bien del imperio: una historia del mundo desde 1945*, pp. 607–8.
3. Investor fear has reached a dramatic climax: in early January 2012, the German government auctioned off 3.9 billion of bonds with negative interest of –0.012%. In other words, investors were paying for the security offered by German debt.
4. S. Alonso, *¿Hablamos del cambio climático?* (Bilbao: Fundación BBVA, 2011).
5. E. Brinkley, "De la industria al conocimiento", in *La Vanguardia Dossier: El declive de Occidente*, 42 (2012): 61 et seq.
6. Jeremy Rifkin says the ICT sector can't be considered a new industrial revolution in its own right. For that to be the case, says the author, ICTs would need to coincide with a new energy system, as occurred in all previous major economic revolutions. See J. Rifkin, "La verdadera crisis económica", *Claves de Razón Práctica*, 216 (2011): 60–6. Rifkin's statement may be appropriate regarding industrial revolutions, but it is not applicable to the broader concept of "economic revolutions". For instance, the great Neolithic revolution would not fit Rifkin's crite-

rion, since it was changes induced by knowledge, biological evolution and intense accumulation of experiences and applied science that enabled the radical transformation of the Neolithic era and the beginnings of economic inactivity. See the classic G. Childe, *Man Makes Himself*, 4th edn. (London: Collins, 1970). Regarding renewable energies see P. Prieto, "Cambio climático y energías renovables", *Ecología Política*, 39 (2010): 73–81.

7. See R. Ayres and B. Warr, *The Economic Growth Engine: How Energy and Work Drive Material Prosperity* (Cheltenham: Edward Elgar, 2009).

8. See J. Sempere and E. Tello (coord.), *El final de la era del petróleo barato* (Barcelona: Icaria, 2007); P. Gómez, *Un planeta en busca de energía* (Madrid: Síntesis, 2007); R. Fernández Durán, *La quiebra de capitalismo global: 2000–2030* (Madrid: Libros en Acción, 2011).

9. A solid defence that extends into applied economics can be found in E. Brinkley. Brinkley talks of "intangible" things linked to R&D, design, computer software, skills and training, which account for 8–10% of GDP in the United States, United Kingdom, Japan, Canada, Sweden, Finland, Denmark, France and Germany. In Spain, they account for only 5–6%.

10. See G. Esping-Andersen, *Social Foundations of Postindustrial Economies* (Oxford: Oxford University Press, 1999); G. Esping-Andersen, *The Three Worlds of Welfare Capitalism* (Cambridge: Polity Press, 1991). The new role of women, as well as preparing children for the knowledge economy, and the crossroads created by the drop in the birth rate and the ageing population are the three vertices that Gøsta Esping-Andersen believes have forced developed countries to review their welfare policies.

11. It is interesting to hear the words of Richard Koo, the chief economist of the Nomura investment bank. He says we are not faced with a fiscal crisis, as has been claimed in Europe, where the most severe austerity measures have been implemented. Instead, Koo argues the Japanese experience should teach us that the current economic woe is a "balance-sheet recession": an obsession to reduce debt that has infiltrated government, families and financial institutions alike at a time when private-sector demand has been stifled. Given this plight, claims the expert, only the public sector is able to turn the situation round, by adopting a clear policy of stimulating the economy. He predicts that the measures taken by Spain could put the country two decades behind in terms of GDP. See *El Pa'is* and *La Vanguardia* on 13 November 2011.

12. Regarding this matter, Robert Skidelsky has said the only global macroeconomic coordination is in one direction: cuts. There is no

coordination to rebuild the economy, since there is no investment in growth. The world economy, he notes, needs directing more towards domestic sources of growth. He recalls the notion of "compact growth", applied to the G20, an element of coordination set out by the former British prime minister Gordon Brown. This "compact growth" would reform the global monetary system with the aim of bringing an end to the era of strong current-account imbalances, reform the financial system to avoid excess bank loans, and bring about macroeconomic policies aimed at boosting short-term global demand. See R. Skidelsky, "The Boom was the Illusion", *New Statesman*, 13 October 2011, <http://www.newstatesman.com/economy/2011/10/world-growth-china-investment>, accessed 20 July 2012.

13. A. Sen and B. Kliksberg, *Primero la gente* (Barcelona: Deusto, 2007), pp. 14 et seq. For Sen, globalization is neither new nor western. Nor is it a curse. He says globalization has actually contributed to the world's progress and that its active agents are often located far from the West. He gives numerous examples: advanced technology in AD 1000 included paper, printing, crossbows, gunpowder, suspension bridges and compasses, all of which were widespread in China but unknown in other parts of the world. The decimal system was developed in India between the second and sixth centuries and was quickly used by Arab mathematicians. Europe, therefore, would have been much poorer had it vehemently opposed this new knowledge from distant lands. These very simple but very powerful examples show that uncritical, unjustified rejection of globalization does not help the world move forward or become more integrated.

14. See A. Sen and B. Kliksberg, pp. 20–23; G. Soros, *The Age of Fallibility: The Consequences of the War on Terror* (Cambridge, MA: Perseus, 2006); R. Simone, *Il Mostro Mite: Perché l'Occidente non va a sinistra* (Milan: Garzanti Libri, 2009); H.M. Enzensberger, *Brussels, the Gentle Monster: or the Disenfranchisement of Europe* (London: Seagull Books, 2011); J. Nash, "The Bargaining Problem", *Econometrica*, 18/2 (1950): 155–62.

15. A theoretical essay with good practical content that provides in-depth analysis of case studies is found in J. Sempere, *Mejor con menos: Necesidades, explosión consumista y crisis ecológica* (Barcelona: Crítica, 2008).

16. An illustrative example of this is hiring in the Spanish hotel sector during the 2011 summer season. There were fewer jobs than ever before, even though 2011 was one of the best years since the turn of the century in terms of number of visitors, money spent by tourists and

hotel profitability. All forecasts were therefore exceeded. See J.P. Velázquez-Gaztelu, "El turismo mundial deja atrás su calvario", *El País – Negocios*, 15 November 2009.
17. E. Hobsbawm, "War and Peace in the 20th Century", in *London Review of Books*, 24/4 (2002).

Appendix

BALANCES OF PAYMENT, in millions of current US dollars

Year	Greece	France	Germany	Portugal
1971			107	
1972			340	
1973			4,181	
1974			9,085	
1975		2,740	3,097	−755
1976	−929	−3,356	3,746	−1,282
1977	−1,075	−405	3,905	−957
1978	−955	7,064	9,278	−463
1979	−1,886	5,142	−5,387	−54
1980	−2,209	−4,208	−15,622	−1,064
1981	−2,408	−4,811	−5,263	−4,686
1982	−1,892	−12,082	5,535	−3,258
1983	−1,878	−5,166	4,370	−1,632
1984	−2,132	−876	9,244	−623
1985	−3,276	−35	18,021	380
1986	−1,676	2,430	39,138	1,166
1987	−1,223	−4,446	44,842	435
1988	−958	−4,619	54,725	−1,066
1989	−2,561	−4,671	58,032	153
1990	−3,537	−9,944	47,659	−181
1991	−1,574	−6,518	−23,050	−716
1992	−2,140	3,893	−21,578	−184
1993	−747	8,990	−17,561	233
1994	−146	7,415	−29,627	−2,196
1995	−2,864	10,840	−27,897	−132
1996	−4,554	20,561	−11,919	−4,906
1997	−4,860	37,801	−7,817	−6,632
1998		37,699	−13,810	−8,379
1999	−7,295	45,865	−27,044	−10,285
2000	−9,820	22,307	−32,279	−11,595
2001	−9,400	26,191	401	−11,445
2002	−9,582	19,703	41,105	−10,264
2003	−12,804	14,757	46,952	−9,593
2004	−13,476	12,361	128,049	−13,616
2005	−18,233	−13,565	142,810	−17,619
2006	−29,565	−15,452	190,221	−19,523
2007	−44,587	−31,249	263,056	−21,179
2008	−51,313	−52,911	243,289	−29,599

BALANCES OF PAYMENT, in millions of current US dollars

Year	Spain	Turkey	UK	Cyprus	Italy
1970			1,970		816
1971			2,717		1,616
1972			533		1,984
1973			–2,412		–2,841
1974		–561	–7,448		–8,275
1975	3,893	–1,648	–3,465		–635
1976	–4,622	–2,029	–1,380	–27	–2,849
1977	–2,455	–3,140	145	–105	2,347
1978	1,251	–1,265	2,163	–185	6,054
1979	757	–1,413	–783	–240	5,914
1980	–5,580	–3,408	6,862	–258	–10,587
1981	–5,363	–1,936	14,127	–172	–10,467
1982	–4,548	–952	7,985	–178	–7,380
1983	–3,013	–1,923	5,292	–205	699
1984	1,778	–1,439	1,833	–222	–3,190
1985	2,785	–1,013	3,314	–180	–4,084
1986	3,914	–1,465	–1,324	–19	2,462
1987	–263	–806	–12,590	–8	–2,635
1988	–3,795	1,596	–35,326	–108	–7,181
1989	–10,924	938	–43,109	–249	–12,812
1990	–18,009	–2,625	–38,811	–154	–16,479
1991	–19,798	250	–19,022	–420	–24,463
1992	–21,537	–974	–23,204	–638	–29,217
1993	–5,804	–6,433	–17,721	110	7,802
1994	–6,389	2,631	–10,026	74	13,209
1995	–1,967	–2,338	–13,436	–205	25,076
1996	–2,234	–2,437	–10,329	–468	39,999
1997	–830	–2,638	–1,403	–418	32,403
1998	–7,251	2,000	–5,273	291	19,998
1999	–18,080	–925	–35,407	–170	8,111
2000	–23,185	–9,920	–38,800	–488	–5,781
2001	–24,064	3,760	–30,281	–322	–652
2002	–22,239	–626	–27,858	–379	–9,369
2003	–30,885	–7,515	–30,002	–292	–19,407
2004	–54,865	–14,431	–45,936	–827	–16,456
2005	–83,388	–22,137	–59,132	–971	–29,713
2006	–110,874	–31,893	–83,077	–1,279	–48,045
2007	–144,657	–37,697	–78,765	–2,595	–51,032
2008	–154,184	–41,685		–4,479	–78,029

TRADE AND SERVICES BALANCE, in millions of current US dollars

Year	Spain	Turkey	UK	Cyprus	Italy
1960	3,486		−505		−2,904
1961	2,630		1,127		−3,071
1962	1,895		945		−4,723
1963	662		1,275		−10,421
1964	1,810		−1,808		−4,570
1965	−491		−281		1,463
1966	−1,044		1,074		506
1967	−1,196		−2,090		−2,297
1968	49		250		1,457
1969	22		4,005		−2,440
1970	1,901		4,400		−9,143
1971	4,758		5,689		−6,491
1972	3,292		−187		−8,178
1973	2,015		627		−11,762
1974	−525		5,753		−8,823
1975	−372		8,612	−111	6,165
1976	−1,829		12,465	−112	5,581
1977	3,740		17,347	−158	14,646
1978	7,777		16,074	−165	20,871
1979	6,427		11,603	−178	18,290
1980	6,256		14,529	−167	1,114
1981	12,236		16,262	−116	10,258
1982	13,134		12,780	−157	8,651
1983	18,268		8,532	−151	17,049
1984	25,196		5,836	−183	12,528
1985	22,963		9,930	−150	12,074
1986	16,656		7,443	−66	7,408
1987	8,945	147	5,735	−79	−3,469
1988	2,556	1,271	−9,927	−88	−4,873
1989	−7,783	941	−14,612	−136	−5,326
1990	−11,845	−491	−7,715	−134	−10,734
1991	−14,544	39	−765	−255	−19,165
1992	−15,012	49	−4,406	−288	−20,718
1993	−3,532	−1,865	−2,792	−40	21,831
1994	678	1,286	2,615	−30	27,469
1995	−967	−175	9,675		37,294
1996	627	−79	8,796		42,386
1997	2,849	−469	6,395		35,045
1998	−6,491	812	−7,456		18,845
1999	−16,918	−261	−17,957		4,504
2000	−19,714	−1,090	−19,361		11,140

2001	−21,209	3,632	−25,210	14,088
2002	−25,399	2,136	−36,890	3,906
2003	−31,945	−236	−38,390	−6,338
2004	−46,016	−2,067	−45,910	−4,410
2005	−60,316	−3,195	−46,076	−8,227
2006	−72,074	−3,468	−47,654	−7,751
2007	−79,784	−4,658	−54,549	−5,922

TRADE AND SERVICES BALANCE, in millions of current US dollars

Year	Greece	France	Germany	Portugal
1960	−1,158	454		239
1961	−1,281	−61		−571
1962	−1,413	−1,628		350
1963	−1,774	−4,115		37
1964	−2,283	−7,650		460
1965	−2,918	−4,421		588
1966	−2,204	−6,507		1,103
1967	−2,417	−7,481		1,695
1968	−2,989	−10,075		−332
1969	−3,477	−13,987		−680
1970	−3,492	−9,020	−13,989	−863
1971	−3,387	−7,689	−21,790	−1,309
1972	−3,483	−11,137	−23,610	−970
1973	−4,878	−15,600	−14,095	−1,859
1974	−3,122	−12,023	4,272	−3,876
1975	−2,563	−3,747	−12,052	−2,134
1976	−2,452	−14,553	−14,373	−2,434
1977	−3,028	−7,594	−14,264	−3,135
1978	−2,476	−5,269	−20,289	−2,508
1979	1,784	−5,803	−31,603	−1,245
1980	−1,738	−8,950	−27,573	−1,815
1981	−1,586	−34	−4,117	−2,570
1982	−3,583	−6,760	6,606	−2,589
1983	−4,709	4,037	−1,129	−351
1984	−3,098	9,621	7,626	1,588
1985	−3,569	6,061	17,114	2,312
1986	−3,676	−5,282	4,930	1,260
1987	−3,175	−13,197	−5,754	−251
1988	−4,937	−14,807	−5,531	−1,953
1989	−6,804	−12,636	−895	−916
1990	−9,283	−14,989	927	−2,079
1991	−10,092	−8,669	1,486	−3,596
1992	−8,750	415	−13,055	−5,679
1993	−9,381	8,637	−13,266	−5,486
1994	−8,499	8,207	−15,253	−6,069
1995	−10,369	12,027	−16,947	−6,171
1996	−11,769	16,541	−6,309	−6,339
1997	−12,270	32,081	9,738	−8,005
1998	−14,357	24,828	2,758	−10,855
1999	−15,738	19,259	−11,937	−13,632
2000	−18,395	13,015	7,250	−13,315

2001	−16,304	14,676	43,204	−13,097
2002	−18,749	13,940	84,608	−12,202
2003	−22,258	4,098	66,960	−10,339
2004	−24,044	−8,916	93,808	−12,075
2005	−23,369	−21,777	103,855	−13,099
2006	−26,689	−26,332	127,480	−11,828
2007	−28,953	−39,246	164,088	−11,645

GILOBALGDP, 1970–2010
(Source: IMF)

Year	Growth
1970	5.02
1971	4.56
1972	5.55
1973	6.86
1974	2.75
1975	1.74
1976	5.38
1977	4.33
1978	4.50
1979	3.76
1980	2.02
1981	2.21
1982	0.89
1983	2.80
1984	4.59
1985	3.64
1986	3.48
1987	3.69
1988	4.49
1989	3.71
1990	2.94
1991	1.47
1992	2.03
1993	2.01
1994	3.38
1995	3.27
1996	3.74
1997	4.04
1998	2.54
1999	3.53
2000	4.70
2001	2.20
2002	2.83
2003	3.63
2004	4.94
2005	4.45
2006	5.07
2007	5.15
2008	3.0
2009	-0.5
2010	5.3

Bibliography

AHAMED, L., *Lords of Finance: the Bankers who Broke the World* (London: William Heinemann, 2009).

AKERLOF, G.A., "The Market for 'Lemons': Quality Uncertainty and the Market Mechanism", *Quarterly Journal of Economics*, 84/ 3 (August 1970), 488–500.

—— and SHILLER, R.J., *Animal Spirits* (Princeton, NJ: Princeton University Press, 2009).

—— DICKENS, W. and PERRY, G., "The Macroeconomics of Low Inflation", *Brookings Papers on Economics Activity*, 1 (1996): 1–76.

ALENYÀ, M. and NAVINÉS, F. (coords.), *L'economia balear: 1970–2010*, Institut Balear d'Economia (Palma: Govern de les Illes Balears, 2010).

ALESINA, A. and GIAVAZZI, F., *El futuro de Europa. Reforma o declive* (Barcelona: Antoni Bosch Editor, 2009).

ALONSO, D. ET AL., *Evolución del sistema fiscal español: 1978–2010* (Madrid: Instituto de Estudios Fiscales, 2011).

ALONSO, S., *¿Hablamos del cambio climático?* (Bilbao: Fundación BBVA, 2011).

ÁLVAREZ, S. and CARPINTERO, O. (eds.), *Economía ecológica: reflexiones y perspectivas* (Madrid: Círculo de Bellas Artes, 2009).

AMIN, S., GUNDER FRANK, A. and JAFFE, H., *¿Cómo será 1984?: debate sobre la crisis y las tendencias actuales del capitalismo mundial* (Madrid: Zero, 1976).

—— ET AL., *Crisis financiera, económica, sistémica* (Madrid: Maia Ediciones, 2010).

ARNSPERGER, C. and VAN PARIJS, P., *Éthique économique et sociale* (Paris: La Découverte & Syros, 2000).

ARRIGHI, G., *Adam Smith in Beijing: Lineages of the Twenty-First Century* (London: Verso, 2007).

ARROW, K.J. and DEBREU, G., "The Existence of an Equilibrium for a Competitive Economy", *Econometrica*, 22 (1954): 265–90.

AYRES, R. and WARR, B., *The Economic Growth Engine: How Energy and Work Drive Material Prosperity* (Cheltenham: Edward Elgar, 2009).

BADE, K., *Migration in European History* (Oxford: Blackwell, 2003).

BARAN, P. and SWEEZY, P., *Monopoly Capital: An Essay on the American*

Economic and Social Order (New York: Monthly Review Press, 1966).

BASALLA, G., *The Evolution of Technology* (Cambridge: Cambridge University Press, 1990). Bateman, V.N, "The Evolution of Markets in Early Modern Europe, 1350–1800: A Study of Grain Prices", *The Economic History Review*, 64/2 (2011): 447–71.

BAUMAN, Z., *44 Letters from the Liquid Modern World* (Cambridge: Polity, 2010).

—— *Collateral Damage: Social Inequalities in a Global Age* (Cambridge: Polity, 2011).

BAUMOL, W.J., "Productivity Policy in the Service Sector", in R. Inman (ed.), *Managing the Service Economy: Prospects and Problems* (Cambridge: Cambridge University Press, 1985).

BENTOLILA, S. ET AL., *La crisis de la economia española* (Madrid: Fedea, 2010).

BERNANKE, B., *Essays on the Great Depression* (Princeton, NJ: Princeton University Press, 2000).

BHADURI, A., *Development with Dignity: A Case for Full Employment* (New Delhi: National Book Trust, 2005).

BHIDÉ, A., *The Origin and Evolution of New Businesses* (Oxford: Oxford University Press, 2003).

BLANCHARD O., DELL'ARICCIA G. and MAURO P., *Rethinking Macroeconomic Policy*, International Monetary Fund Staff Position Note, 12 February 2010, SPN/10/03.

BLAUG, M., *Great Economists since Keynes* (Cheltenham: Edward Elgar, 1998).

BODOMO, A., *La globalización de las inversiones en África* (Madrid: Catarata, 2011).

BOWLES, S. Gordon D.M. and WEISSKOPF, T.E., *After the Waste Land: A Democratic Economics for the Year 2000* (Armonk, NY: M.E. Sharpe, 1991).

BRECHT, B., *Writing the Truth: Five Difficulties* (New York: Grove Press, 1966).

BRENNER, R. "Agrarian Class Structure and Economic Development in Pre-Industrial Europe", *Past and Present*, 70 (1976): 30–75.

—— *The Economics of Global Turbulence: The Advanced Capitalist Economies from Long Boom to Long Downturn, 1945–2005* (New York: Verso, 2006).

—— *The Boom and the Bubble: The US in the World Economy* (New York: Verso, 2002).

—— *Merchants and Revolution: Commercial Change, Political Conflict, and London's Overseas Traders, 1550–1653* (Princeton, NJ: Princeton University Press, 1993).

BRINKLEY, E., "De la industria al conocimiento", in *La Vanguardia Dossier: El declive de Occidente*, 42 (2012), pp. 61 et seq.

BURDEKIN, R.C.K. and SIKLOS, P.L., *Deflation: Current and Historical Perspectives* (Cambridge: Cambridge University Press, 2004).

CABALLERO, G. and GARZA, M.D. (eds.), *La Gran Recesión: Perspectivas globales y regionales* (Coruña: Netbiblo, 2010).

CAFAGNA, L., *Dualismo e sviluppo nella Storia d'Italia* (Venice: Marsilio, 1989).

CALDWELL, B., "Hayek, Friedrich August von (1899–1992)" in Durlauf, S.N. and Blume, L.E. (eds.), *The New Palgrave Dictionary of Economics*, 2nd edn. (Basingstoke: Palgrave Macmillan, 2008).

CAPELLO, R., "La economía regional tras cincuenta años: desarrollos técnicos recientes y desafíos futuros", *Investigaciones Regionales*, 9 (2006): 171–94.

CARBAJO, A., "Ortodoxias y heterodoxias sobre la crisis financiera", *Revista de Libros*, 169 (2011): 3–7.

CARPINTERO, O., *La Bioeconomía de Georgescu-Roegen* (Barcelona: Montesinos, 2006).

CASTELLS, M., *The Rise of the Network Society*, 2nd edn., The Information Age: Economy, Society and Culture, i (Cambridge, MA: Blackwell, 2000).

—— *The Power of Identity*, 2nd edn., The Information Age: Economy, Society and Culture, ii (Cambridge, MA: Blackwell, 2004).

—— *End of Millenium*, 2nd edn., The Information Age: Economy, Society and Culture, iii (Cambridge, MA: Blackwell, 2000).

CEREIJO, E and VELÁZQUEZ, F.J., *El stock de gasto público en los países de la OCDE* (Madrid: FUNCAS, 2008).

CHANDLER, A.D., *The Visible Hand: The Managerial Revolution in American Business* (Cambridge, MA: Harvard University Press, 1977).

CHANG, H., *Bad Samaritans: Rich Nations, Poor Policies and the Threat to the Developing World* (London: Random House, 2007).

—— *Kicking Away the Ladder. Development Strategy in Historical Perspective* (London: Anthem, 2002).

CHILDE, G., *Man Makes Himself*, 4th edn. (London: Collins, 1970).

CHORAFAS, D.N., *Capitalism without Capital* (Basingstoke: Palgrave Macmillan, 2009).

COMÍN, F., *Historia económica mundial* (Madrid: Alianza Editorial, 2011).

COSTAS, A. (coord.), *La crisis de 2008: De la economía a la política y más allá*, Mediterráneo Económico, 18 (2010).

—— "Enseñanzas de la crisis de 2008", in A. Furió et al., *Las crisis a lo largo de la Historia* (Valladolid: Universidad de Valladolid, 2010), 193–237.

—— and ARIAS, X.C., *La torre de la arrogancia: Políticas y mercados después de la tormenta* (Barcelona: Ariel, 2011).

de la Dehesa, G., *La primera gran crisis financiera del siglo XXI* (Madrid: Alianza, 2010).

BRADFORD DELONG, J., "Economics in Crisis", *Project Syndicate*, <http://www.project-syndicate.org/commentary/economics-in-crisis>, accessed 26 August 2012.

DOBB, M., *Capitalismo, crecimiento económico y subdesarrollo* (Barcelona: Oikos Tau, 1975).

DUMÉNIL, G. and LÉVY, D., *Capital Resurgent: Roots of the Neoliberal Revolution* (Cambridge, MA: Harvard University Press, 2007).

DUNGEY, M. ET AL., *Transmission of Financial Crises and Contagion* (Oxford: Oxford University Press, 2011).

EICHENGREEN, B. *Globalizing Capital: A History of the International Monetary System*, 2nd edn. (Princeton, NJ: Princeton University Press, 2008).

—— *Financial Crises and What to Do About Them* (Oxford: Oxford University Press, 2009).

—— "The Great Recession and the Great Depression: Reflections and Lessons", working paper 593, Central Bank of Chile (2010).

—— "The Slide to Protectionism in the Great Depression: Who Succumbed and Why", working paper 15142, National Bureau of Economic Research (2010).

—— and O'ROURKE, K., *A Tale of Two Depressions*, VoxEU.org Ebook, 8 March 2010, <http://www.voxeu.org/article/tale-two-depressions-what-do-new-data-tell-us-february-2010-update>, accessed 26 August 2012.

ENZENSBERGER, H.M., *Brussels, the Gentle Monster: or the Disenfranchisement of Europe* (London: Seagull Books, 2011).

ESPING-ANDERSEN, G., *The Three Worlds of Welfare Capitalism* (Cambridge: Polity Press, 1991).

—— *Social Foundations of Postindustrial Economies* (Oxford: Oxford University Press, 1999).

FELIU, G and SUDRIÀ, C., *Introducció a la història econòmica mundial* (Universitat de València–Universitat de Barcelona, 2006).

FERNÁNDEZ Durán, R., *La quiebra de capitalismo global: 2000–2030* (Madrid: Libros en Acción, 2011).

FISCHER, D.H., *The Great Wave. Price Revolutions and the Rhythm of History* (Oxford: Oxford University Press, 1996).

FONTANA, J., *Europa ante el espejo* (Barcelona: Crítica, 1994).

—— "El triunfo del capitalismo realmente existente", *Claves de Razón Práctica*, 217 (2011): 10–16.

—— *Por el bien del imperio: una historia del mundo desde 1945* (Barcelona: Pasado y Presente, 2011).

FRIEDEN, J.A., *Global Capitalism: Its Fall and Rise in the Twentieth Century* (New York: W.W. Norton, 2006).

FRIEDMAN, M. and SCHWARTZ, A., *A Monetary History of the United States, 1867–1960* (Princeton, NJ: Princeton University Press, 1963).

FUJITA, M., KRUGMAN, P. and VENABLES, A.J., *The Spatial Economy: Cities, Regions, and International Trade* (Cambridge, MA: Massachusetts Institute of Technology, 2000).

FUMAGALLI, A. and MEZZADRA, S. (eds.), *Crisis in the Global Economy: Financial Markets, Social Struggles, and New Political Scenarios* (New York: Semiotexte, 2010).

GALBRAITH, J.K., *The Economics of Innocent Fraud: Truth for our Time* (London: Penguin Books, 2004).

GALINDO, M.A. and MALGESINI, G., "Crecimiento económico: Principales teorías desde Keynes", *Cuadernos*, 25 (1993): 61–8.

GARCÍA MONTALVO, J., *De la quimera inmobiliaria al colapso financiero* (Barcelona: Antoni Bosch Editor, 2009).

GERSCHENKRON, A., *Economic Backwardness in Historical Perspective: A Book of Essays* (Belknap Press of Harvard University Press , Cambridge, MA, 1962).

GINER, S., *El futuro del capitalismo* (Barcelona: Península, 2010).

GLYN, A., *Capitalism Unleashed: Finance, Globalization, and Welfare* (New York: Oxford University Press, 2006).

GÓMEZ, P., *Un planeta en busca de energía* (Madrid: Síntesis, 2007).

GUNDERSON, G., *A New Economic History of America* (New York: McGraw-Hill, 1976).

HARVEY, D., *A Brief History of Neoliberalism* (Oxford: Oxford University Press, 2007).

HEIKKINEN, S. and HJERPPE, R., "The Growth of Finnish Industry in 1860–1913: Causes and Linkages", in P.K. O'Brien (ed.), *The Industrial Revolutions. The Industrial Revolution in Europe*, II (Oxford: Blackwell, 1994), 363–80.

HIRSCHMAN, A.O., *The Strategy of Economic Development* (New Haven, CT: Yale University Press, 1958).

—— *A Propensity to Self-Subversion* (Cambridge, MA: Harvard University Press, 1995).

HOBSBAWM, E., *How to Change the World: Tales of Marx and Marxism* (London: Little, Brown, 2011).

—— "War and Peace in the 20th Century", in *London Review of Books*, 24/4 (2002).

HODNE, F., "Growth in a Dual Economy: The Norwegian Experience, 1814–1914", in P.K. O'Brien (ed.), *The Industrial Revolutions. The Industrial Revolution in Europe*, XVI (Oxford: Blackwell, 1994), 381–410.

HORIUCHI, A.: "A Bank Crisis in a Bank-Centered Financial System: The Japanese Experience since the 1990s", working paper, Chuo University.

HYMAN, S., *Marriner S. Eccles: Private Entrepreneur and Public Servant* (Stanford, Calif.: Stanford University Graduate School of Business, 1976).

JACOBS, M., *The Green Economy: Environment, Sustainable Development and the Politics of the Future* (Concord, MA: Pluto Press, 1991).

JÖRBERG, L., "Structural Change and Economic Growth: Sweden in the 19th Century", in P.K. O'Brien (ed.), *The Industrial Revolutions. The Industrial Revolution in Europe*, II (Oxford: Blackwell, 1994), 412–54.

JUDT, T., *Ill Fares the Land* (New York: Penguin Press, 2010).

KAKU, M., *Physics of the Future: How Science Will Shape Human Destiny and Our Daily Lives by the Year 2100* (New York: Doubleday, 2011).

KALECKI, M., "A Macro-Dynamic Theory of Business Cycles", *Econometrica*, 3 (1935): 327–44.

KEMP, T., *Historical Patterns of Industrialization*, 2nd edn. (London: Longman, 1993).

KINDLEBERGER, C.P., *Keynesianism versus Monetarism and Other Essays in Financial History* (London: HarperCollins, 1985).

—— *The World in Depression, 1929–1939*, rev. and enlarged edn. (Berkeley, Calif.: University of California Press, 1986).

—— *Manias, Panics and Crashes*, 6th edn. (Basingstoke: Palgrave Macmillan, 2011).

KING, J.E., *A History of Post Keynesian Economics since 1936* (Cheltenham: Edward Elgar, 2002).

KJÆRGAARD, T., *The Danish Revolution, 1500–1800: An Ecohistorical Interpretation* (Cambridge: Cambridge University Press, 1994).

KOLB, R.W. (ed.), *Financial Contagion. The Viral Threat to the Wealth of Nations* (Hoboken, NJ: John Wiley & Sons, 2011).

KRUGMAN, P., "Stable Prices and Fast Growth: Just Say No", *The Economist*, 31 August 1996.

—— *The Conscience of a Liberal* (New York: W.W. Norton, 2007).

KRUGMAN, P., *The Great Unraveling: Losing Our Way in the New Century* (New York: W.W. Norton, 2003).

—— *The Return of Depression Economics and the Crisis of 2008* (New York: W.W. Norton, 2009).

—— *The Accidental Theorist and Other Dispatches from the Dismal Science* (New York: W.W. Norton, 1999).

—— *Geography and Trade* (Cambridge, MA: MIT Press, 1991).

LANDES, D., *The Wealth and Poverty of Nations: Why Some Are So Rich and Some So Poor* (New York: W.W. Norton, 1998).

—— *The Unbound Prometheus: Technological Change and Industrial Development in Western Europe from 1750 to the Present*, 2nd edn. (Cambridge: Cambridge University Press, 2003).

—— *Dinastías: Fortunas y desdichas de las grandes familias de negocios* (Barcelona: Crítica, 2006).

LANE, R.E., *The Market Experience* (Cambridge: Cambridge University Press, 1991).

LARDY, N., *Integrating China into the Global Economy* (Washington DC: Brookings Institution Press, 2002).

LATOUCHE, S., *Le pari de la décroissance* (Paris: Fayard, 2006).

LEMOINE, F., *L'économie de la Chine* (Paris: La Découverte, 2003).

LEWIS, M., *The Big Short: Inside the Doomsday Machine* (New York: W.W. Norton, 2010).

LIST, F., *National System of Political Economy* (London: Longmans & Co., 1904).

LLOPIS, E. ET AL., *Historia económica regional de España* (Barcelona: Crítica, 2003).

LÓPEZ, S., "De exploración con Schumpeter", in S. López and J.M. Valdaliso (eds.), *¿Que inventen ellos? Tecnología, empresa y cambio económico en la España contemporánea* (Madrid: Alianza, 1997), 93–4.

LUCAS, A.R., "On the Mechanics of Economic Development", *Journal of Monetary Economics*, 22 (1988): 3–42.

MADDISON, A., *The World Economy: A Millennial Perspective/Historical Statistics* (Paris: OECD Publishing, 1996).

—— *Contours of the World Economy 1–2030 AD: Essays in Macro-Economic History* (Oxford: Oxford University Press, 2007).

MADRICK, J., "Computers: Waiting for the Revolution", *New York Review of Books*, 45/4 (1998): 29–33.

MANERA, C., *L'eixam i les abelles: Per un nou model de creixement a les Illes Balears* (Barcelona: Publicacions de l'Abadia de Montserrat, 2009).

—— *La Recta Raó. Economia, Història Econòmica i Sostenibilitat a les Illes Balears* (Palma: Editorial Moll, 2010).

—— and SANSÓ, A., "The Mediterranean Sea: A Bridge between Coasts:

18th Century Trading Links between the East Coast of Spain ant the Balearic Islands", in S. Cavaciocchi (ed.), *Ricchezza del mare, ricchezza dal mare, secc. XIII–XVIII* (Florence: Le Monnier, 2006), 179–99.

—— JOVER, G. and SANSÓ, A., "Dock Cities and Cointegration Degree of Food Markets in Europe, 1700–1811", working paper, *Third European Congress on World and Global History* (London: London School of Economics, 2011).

—— ET AL., "Políticas de innovación y sus efectos en el cambio de modelo productivo: el caso de las Islas Baleares", working paper, *XII Encuentro de Economistas de Lengua Neolatina, La política para la salida de la crisis: Europa Mediterránea y América Latina en comparación* (Coimbra, 2011).

MARICHAL, C., *A Century of Debt Crises in Latin America: From Independence to the Great Depression, 1820–1930* (Princeton, NJ: Princeton University Press, 1989).

—— *Latinoamérica y España* (Madrid: Marcial Pons, 2009).

—— *Nueva historia de las grandes crisis financieras: Una perspectiva global, 1873–2008* (Barcelona: Debate, 2010).

MARKS, R.B., *The Origins of the Modern World: Fate and Fortune in the Rise of the West*, rev. and updated edn. (Lanham, Md.: Rowman & Littlefield, 2007).

MAROTO, A. and CUADRADO, J.R., *Los cambios estructurales y el papel del sector Servicios en la productividad española*, Servilab, Universidad de Alcalá, document 8/2006.

—— —— "Is Services Growth an Obstacle to Productivity Growth? A Comparative Analysis", *Structural Change & Economic Dynamics*, 20/4 (2009): 254–65

MARTÍN ACEÑA, P. (ed.), *Pasado y presente: De la Gran Depresión del siglo XX a la Gran Recesión del siglo XXI* (Bilbao: Fundación BBVA, 2011).

MARTÍN BELMONTE, S., *Nada está perdido: un sistema monetario y financiero alternativo y sano* (Barcelona: Icaria, 2011).

MARTÍNEZ ALIER, J. and ROCA JUSMET, J. *Economía ecológica y política ambiental* (Mexico: Fondo de Cultura Económica, 2006).

MARX, K., *El Capital* (Mèxic: Siglo XXI, 1975).

MCCLOSKEY, D.N. "The Rhetoric of Economics", *Journal of Economic Literature*, 21/2 (1983): 481–517.

MCPHERSON, M.S. "Hirschman, Albert Otto (born 1915)", in S.N. Durlauf, and L.E. Blume (eds.), *The New Palgrave Dictionary of Economics*, 2nd edn. (Basingstoke: Palgrave Macmillan, 2008).

MELDOLESI, L., *Discovering the Possible: The Surprising World of Albert O. Hirschman* (University of Notre Dame Press: London, c1995).

MINSKY, H., *John Maynard Keynes* (New York: McGraw-Hill, 2008).

—— *Stabilizing an Unstable Economy* (New York: McGraw-Hill, 2008).

MOKYR, J., *The Gifts of Athena: Historical Origins of the Knowledge Economy* (Princeton, NJ: Princeton University Press, 2002).

MUMFORD, L., *Technics and Civilization* (Chicago: University of Chicago Press, 2010).

NAPOLEONI, C., *Smith, Ricardo, Marx: Observations on the History of Economic Thought* (Oxford: Basil Blackwell, 1975).

NAREDO, J.M., *La burbuja inmobiliario-financiera en la coyuntura económica reciente (1985–1995)* (Madrid: Siglo XXI, 1998).

—— "Claves de la globalización financiera y de la presente crisis internacional", *Estudis d'Història Econòmica*, 19 (2002): 201–15.

—— *Raíces económicas del deterioro ecológico y social: Más allá de los dogmas* (Madrid: Siglo XXI, 2006).

NASH, J., "The Bargaining Problem", *Econometrica*, 18/2 (1950): 155–62.

NAVARRO, V., TORRES, J. and GARZÓN A., *Hay alternativas: Propuestas para crear empleo y bienestar social en España* (Madrid: Sequitur, 2011).

NAVINÉS, F., "Algunes reflexions fetes des de l'enfocament clàssic de l'excedent sobre el procés de terciarització i especialització productiva: el cas de Balears" in A. Forcades (ed.), *Repensem el model de creixement balear* (Palma: Cambra de Comerç de Mallorca, Eivissa i Formentera and Cercle d'Economia de Mallorca, 2006).

NUTI, D., "El ciclo político de Kalecki desde una óptica actual. Una introducción", *Revista de Economía Crítica*, 12 (2011): 207–13.

O'CONNOR, J., *Accumulation Crisis* (Oxford: Basit Blackwell, 1984).

OKUN, A.M., *The Political Economy of Prosperity: Possibilities and Problems of a Functional Economic Integration in West Africa* (New York: W.W. Norton, 1970).

OLIVERES, A., *Aturem la crisi: Les perversions d'un sistema que és possible canviar* (Barcelona: Angle Editorial, 2011).

OSTERHAMMLE, J. and PETERSSON, N., *Globalization: A Short History* (Princeton, NJ: Princeton University Press, 2005).

OTTE, M., *Stoppt das Euro-Desaster* (Berlin: Ullstein Buchverlage, 2010).

—— *Die Krise halt sich nicht an Regeln: 99 Fragen zur aktuellen Situation – und wie es weitergeht* (Berlin: Econ, 2010).

PÉREZ, C., *Technological Revolutions and Financial Capital: The Dynamics of Bubbles and Golden Ages* (Cheltenham: Edward Elgar, 2002).

PETRINI, R. *Processo agli economisti* (Milan: Chiarelettere, 2009).

POLANYI, K., *The Great Transformation: The Political and Economic Origins of our Time* (Boston, MA: Beacon Press, 2001).

POLLARD, S., *Marginal Europe: The Contribution of Marginal Lands since the Middle Ages* (Oxford: Oxford University Press, Clarendon Press, 1997).

PRIETO, P., "Cambio climático y energías renovables", *Ecología Política*, 39 (2010): 73–81.

RAJAN, R.G., *Fault Lines: How Hidden Fractures Still Threaten the World Economy* (Princeton, NJ: Princeton University Press, 2010).

REDDY, W.M., *The Rise of Market Culture: The Textile Trade and French Society, 1750–1900* (Cambridge: Cambridge University Press, 1987).

REICH, R.B., "The Great Recession, the Great Recessions and what's ahead", working paper, <http://www.irle.berkeley.edu/conference/2010/materials/reich.pdf>, accessed 17 July 2012.

REINERT, E., *How Rich Countries Got Rich...and Why Poor Countries Stay Poor* (London: Constable, 2007).

REINHART, C.M. and ROGOFF, K.S., *This Time Is Different: Eight Centuries of Financial Folly* (Princeton, NJ: Princeton University Press, 2009).

RENARD, M., *China and its Regions: Economic Growth and Reform in Chinese Provinces* (Edward Elgar: Cheltenham, 2002).

RIFKIN, J., "La verdadera crisis económica", *Claves de Razón Práctica*, 216 (2011): 60–6.

—— *The Third Industrial Revolution: How Lateral Power is Transforming Energy, the Economy, and the World* (New York: Palgrave Macmillan, 2011).

ROBINSON, J. and EATWELL, J., *Introduction to Modern Economics* (London: McGraw-Hill, 1973).

ROMER, P., "Increasing returns and long-run growth", *Journal of Political Economy*, 94 (1986): 1002–37.

—— "Human Capital and Growth: Theory and Evidence", NBER working paper 3173, <http://www.nber.org/papers/w3173>, accessed 17 July 2012.

RONCAGLIA, A., *Why the Economists Got It Wrong: The Crisis and Its Cultural Roots* (London: Anthem Press, 2010).

—— *Il mito della mano invisibile* (Rome: Laterza, 2011).

ROSENBERG, N., *Inside the Black Box: Technology and Economics* (Cambridge: Cambridge University Press, 1982).

ROUBINI, N. and MIHM, S., *Crisis Economics: A Crash Course in the Future of Finance* (New York: Penguin Press, 2010).

ROWLEY, C. and BENSON, J. (eds.), *Globalization and Labour in the Asia Pacific Region* (London: Frank Cass, 2000).

—— FITZGERALD, R. and STEWART, P (eds.), *Managed in Hong Kong:*

Adaptive Systems, Entrepreneurship and Human Resources (London: Frank Cass, 2000).

RUSSELL, B., *Sceptical Essays* (London: Routledge Classics, 2004).

SCHULTZ, T., "Education and Economic Growth", in N. Henry, *Social Forces Influencing American Education* (Chicago: University of Chicago Press, 1961).

—— *Investing in People: The Economics of Population Quality* (Berkeley, Calif.: University of California Press, 1981).

SCHUMPETER, J.A., *Can Capitalism Survive? Creative Destruction and the Future of the Global Economy* (New York: HarperPerennial, 2009).

SEMPERE, J., *Mejor con menos: Necesidades, explosión consumista y crisis ecológica* (Barcelona: Crítica, 2008).

—— and TELLO, E. (coord.), *El final de la era del petróleo barato* (Barcelona: Icaria, 2007).

SEN, A., "Capitalismo más allá de la crisis", *El Viejo Topo*, 255 (2009): 16–23.

—— and KLIKSBERG, B., *Primero la gente* (Barcelona: Deusto, 2007).

SIMONE, R., *Il Mostro Mite: Perché l'Occidente non va a sinistra* (Milan: Garzanti Libri, 2009).

SKIDELSKY, R., "The Boom was the Illusion", *New Statesman*, 13 October 2011, <http://www.newstatesman.com/economy/2011/10/world-growth-china-investment>, accessed 20 July 2012.

—— *The Return of the Master* (London: Allen Lane, 2009).

SMITH, A. *The Theory of Moral Sentiments* (Oxford: Clarendon, 1976).

SOLOW, R.M., "Economics: Is Something Missing?", in W.N. Parker (ed.), *Economic History and the Modern Economist* (Oxford: Basil Blackwell, 1986), 21–9.

—— "How Did Economics Get That Way and What Way Did it Get?", in T. Bender and R.E. Schorske, *American Academic Culture in Transformation: Fifty Years, Four Disciplines* (Princeton, NJ: Princeton University Press, 1998), 57–76.

SORKIN, A.R., *Too Big to Fail: The Inside Story of How Wall Street and Washington Fought to Save the Financial System* (New York: Viking, 2009).

SOROS, G., *The Age of Fallibility: The Consequences of the War on Terror* (Cambridge, MA: Perseus, 2006).

STEINDL, J., *Economic Papers 1941–1988* (London: Macmillan, 1990).

STERN, G. and FELDMAN, R.J., *Too Big to Fail. The Hazards of Bank Bailouts* (Washington: Brookings Institution Press, 2004).

STIGLITZ, J., *Globalization and its Discontents* (New York: W.W. Norton, 2002).

—— *The Roaring Nineties: A New History of the World's Most Prosperous Decade* (New York: W.W. Norton, 2003).

—— *Freefall: America, Free Markets, and the Sinking of the World Economy* (New York: W.W. Norton, 2010).

—— and WEISS, A., "Credit Rationing in Markets with Imperfect Information", *American Economic Review*, 71/3 (1981): 393–410.

STUDWELL, J., *The China Dream: The Elusive Quest for the Greatest Untapped Market on Earth* (London: Profile Books, 2002).

SYLOS LABINI, P., "Le prospettive dell'economia mondiale", *Moneta e Credito*, 223 (2003): 267–95.

—— *Torniamo ai classici. Produttività del lavoro, progresso tecnico e sviluppo economico* (Bari: Laterza, 2005).

SYLLA, R and TONIOLO, G., *Patterns of European Industrialization. The Nineteenth Century* (London: Routledge, 1993).

TAIBO, C., *En defensa del decrecimiento* (Madrid: Catarata, 2009).

TELLO, E., "Apuntes sobre la crisis, o las crisis de nuestro tiempo", published online, <http://www.fundacionbetiko.org>, accessed 17 July 2012.

TEMIN, P., *Lessons from the Great Depression* (Cambridge, MA: MIT Press, 1989).

TOBIN, J., "Arthur M. Okun (1928–1980)", in Durlauf, S.N. and Blume, L.E. (eds.), *The New Palgrave Dictionary of Economics*, 2nd edn. (Basingstoke: Palgrave Macmillan, 2008).

TODD, E., *After the Empire: The Breakdown of the American Order* (New York: Columbia University Press, 2003).

TORNABELL, R., *El día después de la crisis* (Barcelona: Ariel, 2010).

TORRERO, A., "El final de la burbuja especulativa y la crisis econòmica de Japón", in *Observatorio de la Economía y la Sociedad del Japón*, 3 (2011).

—— *La crisis financiera internacional y sus efectos sobre la economía española* (Madrid: Marcial Pons, 2011).

TSUZU, S., *Japan's Capitalism: Creative Defeat and Beyond*, Canto edn. (Cambridge: Cambridge University Press, 1996).

URDANGARIN, C. and ALDABALDETRECU, F., *Historia técnica y económica de la máquina herramienta* (San Sebastián: Caja de Ahorros Provincial de Guipúzcoa, 1982).

DE VRIES, J., "The Limits of Globalization in the Early Modern World", *The Economic History Review*, 63/3 (2009): 710–33.

WALLERSTEIN, I.M., ARRIGHI, G and HOPKINS, T.K., *Antisystemic Movements* (London: Verso, 1989).

WEBER, M., *General Economic History* (Mineola, Tex.: Dover Publications, 2003).

WILLIAMSON, J. and O'ROURKE, K., *Globalization and History: The Evolution of a Nineteenth-Century Atlantic Economy* (Cambridge: Cambridge University Press, 1999).

—— and PAMUK, S., *The Mediterranean Response to Globalization before 1950* (London: Routledge, 2000).

—— BORDO, M. and TAYLOR, A.M. *(eds.)*, *Globalization in Historical Perspective* (Chicago: Chicago University Press, 2006).

—— ROSÉS, J. and O'ROURKE, K., "Globalization, Growth and Distribution in Spain, 1500–1913", working paper 13055, 2008.

WORONOFF, D., *Histoire de l'industrie en France* (Paris: Seuil, 1998).

ZIEGLER, J., *L'Empire de la Honte* (Paris: Fayard, 2005).

Index

Note: Page numbers in italics refer to figures or tables.

About the Author

Carles Manera (Palma, Spain, 1957) holds doctorates in History (University of the Balearic Islands) and Economics (University of Barcelona). He is a professor in History and Economic Institutions at the University of the Balearic Islands in the Department of Applied Economics. Among other awards he received the 2003 Catalonia Prize for Economics. Dr Manera was Vice-Rector of Economic and Administrative Planning of the University of the Balearic Islands from 1996 to 2003, and Economy and Finance Minister for the Balearic Islands government from 2007 to 2011.

Contact: carles.manera@uib.es